Banking in Europe

The Single European market of 1992 will radically affect the operations of the European banking system. As banks prepare for the Single European market, they will need to carefully examine their strategies for gaining and retaining market share in this changing economic environment and to be aware of the threats to independent operation that financial deregulation may bring.

Beginning with an examination of banking in the twelve EC member countries, *Banking in Europe: The Single Market* looks at the implications of removing current financial barriers and considers how a free market in banking might operate within the Community. Relevant EC legislation – including the Second Banking Co-ordination Directive – is examined, illustrating how the problems of deregulation might be addressed. The text then highlights the strategies currently being adopted by banks to develop overseas operations while safeguarding traditional markets and discusses the implications of the recent growth in financial services and the possibility of European monetary and economic union.

Banking in Europe is an invaluable guide for all who are concerned with the changing economic climate in Europe. It will be of particular interest for those students and practitioners of banking and finance who wish to look beyond the present and into the possibilities offered by 'the new Europe'.

Rob Dixon is Principal Lecturer in Financial Management at the Newcastle Business School, Newcastle-upon-Tyne Polytechnic. He is the author of several books on investment and financial management and is a consultant editor for the Stock Exchange's *Financial Services Guide*.

Banking in Europe
The Single Market

Rob Dixon

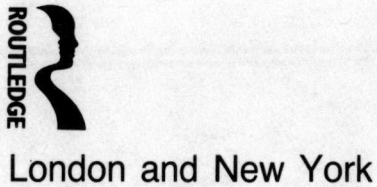

London and New York

First published 1991
by Routledge
11 New Fetter Lane, London EC4P 4EE

Simultaneously published in the USA and Canada
by Routledge
a division of Routledge, Chapman and Hall, Inc.
29 West 35th Street, New York, NY 10001

© 1991 Rob Dixon

Typeset by Columns Design and Production Services
Printed and bound in Great Britain by
Mackays of Chatham PLC, Chatham, Kent

All rights reserved. No part of this book may be reprinted or
reproduced or utilized in any form or by any electronic,
mechanical, or other means, now known or hereafter invented,
including photocopying and recording, or in any information
storage or retrieval system, without permission in writing from
the publishers.

British Library Cataloguing in Publication Data
Dixon, R. (Robert) *1954–*
 Banking in Europe: The Single Market
 1. Europe. Banking
 I. Title
 332.1094

ISBN 0–415–05572–5
ISBN 0–415–05573–3 pbk

Library of Congress Cataloging in Publication Data
Dixon, Rob, 1954–
 Banking in Europe: The Single Market/Rob Dixon
 p. cm.
 Includes bibliographical references and index.
 ISBN 0–415–05572–5 – ISBN 0–415–05573–3 (pbk)
 1. Banks and banking–European Economic Community countries.
 2. Europe 1992. 3. Banking law–European Economic Community
 countries. I. Title.
 HG2980.5.A6D58 1991
 332.1'5'094–dc20   90–43026
                                                             CIP

Contents

List of figures and tables	vii
Preface	ix
List of abbreviations	xi
1 Introduction to banking in the European Community	1
2 The European Community and the single market programme	27
3 The current position and the Commission's approach	46
4 The legislative measures	58
5 Banking strategies for 1992	77
6 Preparations and attitudes of the major UK banks	93
7 Economic aspects of a single market in financial services	99
8 Conclusions	116
Appendix I	122
Appendix II	129
Index	131

Figures and tables

Figures

2.1 UK trade patterns, 1972–89   41

Tables

1.1 Value added in credit and insurance, 1985	25
1.2 Bank loans outstanding as percentage of GNP	25
1.3 EC branches and subsidiaries, 1988	26
4.1 Scope of the Second Banking Directive	59
4.2 Current capital ratios	73
5.1 Overview of payment systems and services in EEC member states, 1986	79
5.2 Cost of consumer credit	80
5.3 Mortgage costs in the EC	81
5.4 Status of top 162 EC banks in 1988	86
7.1 Percentage difference in prices from the average of the four lowest national prices	100
7.2 Gains in consumer surplus	102
7.3 Gains in consumer surplus, banking sector	102
AI.1 European top 50 banks by capital, 1988	122
AI.2 European top 300 banks by country	123
AII.1 Standard financial products surveyed for Cecchini report	129

Preface

The completion of the single market among the European Community members in 1992 will be one of the more significant events of the decade. It will have a profound effect on businesses and industry throughout Europe; not least among the financial services industries of the different member states.

This book examines how European banking and financial business will be affected by the coming of the single market, by examining the existing banking systems of the Community, and by discussing the problems faced by institutions trying to expand into Europe at present. The effect of the legislation passed by the Commission to remove these barriers to free trade is looked at (in particular, the Second Banking Co-ordination Directive), together with the preparations being made by the big European banks to take advantage of this open market.

Taking a slightly wider view, the economic aspects of a single financial market on Europe and European business are considered, as are the moves towards economic and monetary union, proposed by the Delors Committee report.

This book was written with practitioners and students of banking in mind, in order to give them a comprehensive and clear overview of banking in Europe, and to show how the industry might be affected by the internal market. And it is hoped that those involved in banking, as well as the more general reader, will find this work to be both interesting and informative.

Finally, the author wishes to express his thanks to Carolyne Jones and Charlotte Ridings, who helped with the early research, drafting, typing and proof-reading of this book.

Abbreviations

ACP	African, Caribbean, Pacific
ATM	Automated Teller Machines
BBA	British Banking Association
CD	Certificates of Deposit
DTB	Deutsche Terminborse
ECPS	European Council for Payments Systems
ECSC	European Coal and Steel Community
EDP	Electronic Data Processing
EEC	European Economic Community
EFTA	European Free Trade Association
EFTPOS	Electronic Funds Transfer at Point Of Sale
EIB	European Investment Bank
EMCF	European Monetary Co-operation Fund
EMS	European Monetary System
EMU	Economic and Monetary Union
ERM	Exchange Rate Mechanism
ESCB	European System of Central Banks
Euratom	European Atomic Energy Community
GATT	General Agreement on Tariffs and Trade
GDP	Gross Domestic Product
GNP	Gross National Product
G10	Group of 10
G30	Group of 30
IFSC	International Financial Services Centre
LIFFE	London International Financial Futures Exchange
M & A	Mergers and acquisitions

MATIF	Marché à Terme des Instruments Financiers
PCI	Public credit institutions
SEA	Single European Act
TAURUS	Transfer and automated registration of uncertificated stock

Chapter 1

Introduction to banking in the European Community

OVERVIEW OF THE EC BANKING INDUSTRY

Banking practices and customs vary widely from one Community country to another, as do the markets in which the diverse financial institutions operate. The banking systems of the member states are discussed below, together with the other, related, financial industries in each country. Banks are becoming increasingly involved in these related industries (such as insurance, securities trading, etc.) and therefore these are discussed too.

The British banking system

The UK banking system is probably the most developed and sophisticated in the European Community. It is a very open system, with no restrictions on foreign banks operating in it, and since 1986 banks have been able to participate freely in the securities business as well.

There are two main categories of bank: clearing banks and merchant banks. The clearing banks dominate the market. Traditionally, they have handled most of the country's cheque accounts and credit facilities. The largest of these banks are the 'Big Four' London-based banks − National Westminster, Barclays, Midland and Lloyds. These, together with the Scottish clearing banks (the largest of which are the Royal

Bank of Scotland and the Bank of Scotland) have a branch network of 13,000 outlets, and are the main providers of banking services to the public. Most of the clearing banks' business is done in the retail market, and they offer a very wide range of services to their customers, from simple cheque accounts to mortgages, pensions, loans and investment plans and advice. Their subsidiaries tend to concentrate on providing specialized services to large corporate customers.

The merchant banks operate in the wholesale market, and so do not have branch networks. Their main business is providing corporate finance, but they also give companies other services, such as investment management and financial advice. The merchant banks are mainly subsidiaries of the clearing banks, but the leading 16 are separate accepting houses, which operate on the discount money market.

The Trustee Savings Bank (TSB) is the other main bank in the UK. This is an amalgamation of what were originally non-profit-making thrift institutions. In 1976 the restrictions on their operations were lifted, and now the TSB is able to offer a normal range of banking services in the retail market. It also owns one of the major finance houses. Two public banking institutions exist as well, operating through the Post Office. These are the National Savings Bank, which provides deposit and cash withdrawal facilities, with deposits being invested in government securities, and the National Girobank. This mainly provides a money transmission service. Neither of these two institutions has a significant share of the deposit market.

The banking market is extremely competitive, especially the retail market, where the clearing banks not only compete with each other but also have recently been facing strong challenges from the UK building societies. Traditionally, these took in household savings and gave mortgages. However, the Building Societies Act of 1986 removed most of the previous restrictions on the activities the societies could carry out. Since then the building societies have been operating current cheque accounts, issuing credit cards and personal loans, and offering pensions, unit trusts and share dealing facilities to their customers. Their innovations, such as paying interest on current accounts, have forced the clearing banks to follow suit. The banks can expect even more competition from the building societies, now that building societies have been allowed to convert from mutual societies to plcs.

The banks' response to these challenges has been to diversify as well. They have moved successfully into the mortgage market (Lloyds setting up their own chain of estate agents), although the current decline of the market may hit them fairly hard, and into life assurance (Lloyds, again, has linked up with the life assurance firm Abbey Life to offer their policies).

The majority of the large banks have, in fact, linked up with insurance companies in this way, following the Financial Services Act. This requires insurance sellers either to act as totally independent brokers, or to act exclusively for one company. Of the big banks, only Nat West has chosen the first option; the other three have tied up with insurance companies, such as Commercial Union (Midland), and, as was said previously, Abbey Life (Lloyds).

The domestic banks also face competition in the wholesale market from the large number of foreign banks operating in the country. At the beginning of 1989 there were 521 foreign banks (including consortium banks) represented in London. These banks also participate in the money markets, especially the Eurocurrency market centred on London.

The foreign banks have been attracted to London because the UK financial market is one of the most open and deregulated in the world, ranking behind New York and Tokyo in importance. All exchange controls were abolished in 1979, and in a major development in 1986 ('Big Bang') the Stock Exchange was opened up by the abandonment of the single capacity system of trading (whereby the duties of brokers and market makers were segregated) in favour of the more normal dual capacity system. This has allowed all the banks (domestic and foreign) to participate more directly in the Exchange. A full range of bonds and hedging instruments (such as financial futures and options), with a variety of maturities, is available on the different markets.

The UK financial markets are not without their problems, however, some of which were highlighted by the stock market Crash of 1987. For example, the Stock Exchange still relies on a manual clearing and settlement system for equity transactions – a slow, laborious and antiquated process, described by one dealer as being not archaic, but neolithic. The average settlement time for deals is five to six weeks (although, for some, it can be up to three months). This does not compare very well with other major exchanges, both European and worldwide. For these the average period is nearer two to three weeks.

The G30 Committee has demanded that action should be taken by its members to improve the stability of the financial markets in the wake of the Crash, one of the measures being the adoption of paperless clearing systems. This is because the longer the settlement periods are, the more the risk to which dealers are exposed. London, therefore, has proposed to implement such a system (TAURUS – 'transfer and automated registration of uncertificated stock') by 1993. An added incentive to meet this deadline was provided by the Chancellor in his 1990 Budget: the abolition of stamp duty on UK security transactions when (and only when!) TAURUS comes into operation.

The Stock Exchange has also just announced plans to reorganize its divisions to improve efficiency. In March 1990 plans were published for the creation of four operating divisions: primary markets, secondary markets, settlement services, and the London Traded Options Market (although this has since merged with LIFFE, the London International Financial Futures Exchange).

Greater efficiency is certainly needed if London's position is not going to be seriously challenged by Frankfurt or Paris, which are both growing far more quickly than London in terms of daily volumes of stock traded. If London's Exchange does not innovate, and relies too much upon its past record, it could find itself loosing out to these newer financial centres.

The other EC banking systems

Belgium

There are three groups of major financial institutions in Belgium: the commercial banks, which are all privately owned; the private savings banks; and the state-owned public credit institutions. The commercial banks carry out a wide range of activities, and dominate the lending market. The three largest are Générale Bank, Banque Bruxelles Lambert, and Krediet-bank. The savings banks specialize in domestic loans and savings, and the six PCIs provide specific funding (such as mortgage credit) on advantageous terms, although they are now becoming less specialized. They also accounted for just over 40 per cent of domestic savings in 1987. There are plans to combine these six PCIs into two large bank groups.

The sector is concentrated and overbanked, with a total of 86 banks in a domestic market of only 10 million, and a ratio of one branch per 1,000 people. This, however, has encouraged competition, especially in the areas of short-term credit and finance for small/medium-sized businesses, with the larger savings banks moving into the traditional territory of the commercial banks, capitalizing on their customer loyalty, large branch networks and low cost of funding.

Belgian banking is the most internationalized in Europe, barring Luxembourg and the UK: 61 of the 86 banks operating in the country are foreign. This internationalization is given added impetus by the absence of controls on capital movements and by incentives of tax breaks for foreign institutions setting up branches in Belgium. Foreign currency accounted for 57 per cent of the deposit banks' total assets in 1987, and for nearly 71 per cent of their total liabilities. This was due to the banks' strong encouragement of private ECU usage, and to their 9.3 per cent share of the European market in Eurocurrency deposits.

The market for life insurance is extremely concentrated, with the largest insurance company cornering 22 per cent of it. The non-life market is rather more open, however. Some of the largest insurance companies operating in Belgium are Swiss and American.

The mortgage market is also concentrated, with the state-owned savings bank ASLK-CGER providing a third of all house credit. Most of the rest of the market is supplied, rather naturally, by the other savings banks. Loans can be obtained for between 60 and 100 per cent of the value of the property, at a fixed rate of interest, although ASLK-CGER has been considering introducing loans with interest rates which can be varied every five years.

Belgian banks do face problems and restrictions. ASLK-CGER, in particular, has its competitiveness hampered by the requirement that it provides BFr 1 billion annually for social services projects. The banks in general are not permitted to hold shares in commercial companies, unless they are other credit institutions, and they have the highest wage structure in Europe, pushing up costs, together with very short working hours. Productivity has been improved recently, however, by the use of low staff numbers and EDP management. The sector also suffers from comparatively low rates of return on its business and a lack of equity capital. The most disliked regulation is a 25 per cent withholding tax, which dissuades foreigners from investing in government funds, bonds and bank savings.

The government began to take steps to modernize the financial markets in May 1988. This modernization has entailed opening up the brokerage system to credit institutions and insurance companies, breaking the monopoly of the brokers, and introducing some new financial instruments. Before modernization there was no financial futures market and a very limited range of debt instruments. The style of dealing on the stock market has also been revamped. Previously, dealing was carried out through a daily two-hour auction system. Now there is 24-hour electronic trading via the same centralized system used in Paris and Toronto: computer-assisted trading systems (CATS). Securities from 30 Belgian companies and 70 internationals are traded on the system. The purpose behind CATS was to reduce the amount of stock traded over the counter.

Denmark

The Danish banking market is one of the more open and competitive in the EC. It was opened up to foreign banks ten years ago, and all foreign exchange controls were removed in 1988. Seventy commercial banks and 140 savings banks (which are allowed to offer the same, universal banking service as the commercial banks) serve a very small domestic population of just 5.2 million people. Most of these banks are small, town ones. There are about 15–20 regional bank networks, and only a handful of the banks have a national network. The commercial banks dominate the basic lending and deposit sectors, with over 70 per cent of the market, but the largest three commercial banks have a combined market share of under 40 per cent.

The small local and regional banks tend to cater for the retail banking market. The larger banks specialize in merchant banking and corporate finance. However, the banks are experiencing increasing competition. For example, insurance companies are diversifying into traditional bank areas, such as consumer lending and project finance. The banks, in turn, are expanding into pension and insurance provision, and so the edges between the financial specialisms are increasingly being blurred.

Another area the larger banks are expanding into is mortgage credit. Until October 1989 three credit institutions had a monopoly over this area, but now banks are allowed to issue mortgage bonds for borrowers as well. The bonds are issued against the value of the property, rather than against the borrower's creditworthiness, which makes it easier to get a mortgage in Denmark than in any other member state: 60 per cent of houses are owner-occupied. However, the market has been loosing its attraction – tax changes have encouraged more people to save, and property values have been falling. The margins on the business are also very low, at about 0.5 per cent.

The Stock Exchange has been reformed recently to allow banks to participate in it. Before, 24 broking companies had a monopoly over trading, but now both banks and insurance companies can set up their own limited liability brokerage companies and trade on the Exchange. Modernization has taken place too. Securities used to be traded under an auction system, but in 1988 the Exchange was computerized and became the first one in Europe to trade, clear and settle futures, bonds, equities and options on the same on-line system. Denmark's bond market ranks among the world's top ten by volume, with about 2,000 bonds quoted on the Exchange. About 60 per cent of these are mortgage bonds, with another 35 per cent issued by the government.

In spite of the openness of its markets and the sophistication of its Stock Exchange trading, Denmark has several drawbacks which prevent it becoming an international financial centre. Foreign banks still have only 1 per cent of the market, because of high rates of corporation tax (50 per cent, compared with the

UK's 35 per cent), high labour and other costs, tough capital requirements (a ratio of 8 per cent on liabilities, rather than on the more normal risk-weighted assets), and a lack of large companies. Currently, most foreign banks are also not allowed to set up brokerage companies; only those from the other Nordic countries can do so. Danish banks are too small at present to compete with the larger foreign banks in Europe either (only one Danish bank ranks among the top 50 in Europe by capital), although there have been some mergers between them to increase their competitiveness. (Hostile takeover bids are barred, as banks can only hold a 30 per cent stake in another bank.)

France

Ninety-nine per cent of French adults have accounts with either a commercial or a savings bank, and 95 per cent of them have cheque accounts. They are served by over 26,000 branches, one of the highest number of branches per capita in Europe. The market is dominated by a few very large banks; for example, the commercial banks Banque Nationale de Paris, Crédit Lyonnaise and Société Générale, and the co-operative Crédit Agricole. Since 1984 the banks have been able to offer a universal banking service; before that the deposit, investment and credit banks were kept strictly separate. Many of the banks are state controlled, although some of the largest ones have now been privatized.

Because of the saturation of the market for traditional bank accounts, banks are moving into other areas, offering new products and services, creating something of a boom in the retail market, and expanding overseas. One of these areas is the life assurance market, which the banks have been moving into recently through subsidiary insurance companies. By 1989 the banks had captured 40 per cent of this market, together with 75 per cent of the retirement savings schemes market. The mutual banks have a significant share of the non-life insurance market too.

The mortgage market is still comparatively undeveloped at present. The major lenders are the savings banks, with competition limited because there are no independent mortgage brokers. Lending rates are set by the authorities, and deposits of up to 40 per cent of the house price can be required. Sometimes the savings banks will lend at reduced start-up rates to people who already save with them. The interest rates are generally fixed; adjustable rates are available, but the banks are permitted to lend only a certain amount of mortgage finance at variable interest rates.

Credit card usage in France is high, with 8 million Visa and Mastercards circulating. The banks are trying to cut down on their costs by encouraging people to use cards instead of cheques. To do this they have issued 7.5 million unified bank cards as well, which are acceptable in 460,000 outlets and 11,200 ATMs.

Despite the existence of some exchange controls and restrictions on banking practices (for example, interest cannot be given on current accounts and, therefore, banks cannot charge for many services), there are 168 foreign banks operating in France – one of the largest numbers behind London and New York. Recent reforms of the stock exchange are the main reason for this growth and internationalization of the French financial markets.

The modernization of the Bourse was begun in 1986. A continuous electronic trading system (CAC) replaced the system of two-hour trading sessions and the daily fixing of stock prices. This in turn has been replaced by a more powerful and updated system, CAC II. Brokers' fixed commissions have been abolished, although their monopoly over trading will not end until 1992. New money market instruments have been introduced, such as certificates of deposit, commercial paper and new treasury bills, with a variety of maturities and denominations. New markets have been established too. In 1986 a futures market, the Marché à Terme des Instruments Financiers (MATIF) was set up, and in 1988 a market in traded options on futures began, giving investors a range of hedging and arbitrage opportunities. One Paris broker summed up the changes: 'In three years Paris has been transformed from a mickey-mouse outfit into something to challenge the rest of the world' (*The Banker*, March 1988). The full internationalization of the French financial markets will not, however, be complete until the remaining restrictions, especially those on capital movements, are abolished.

West Germany

West German banking is fairly unconcentrated, but it is very overbanked. Four and a half thousand banks have a retail network of about 44,000 branches – one branch for every 1,350 Germans. There are two groups of financial institutions: specialized credit institutions (such as mortgage banks and savings banks), and universal banks, offering services in the securities, retail and investment sectors. This group of banks includes the 'Big Three' – Deutsche Bank, Dresdner Bank and Commerzbank – together with regional banks (the *Landesbanks*, the regional parents of the savings banks) and co-operative regional institutions. Unlike other European countries, universal banking is compulsory in Germany. A bank will not get a banking licence unless it offers a complete range of services.

The overlapping of the services that the different institutions provide creates fierce competition, especially as the banks' income has been dropping recently, with savers moving out of the traditional bank savings accounts and into higher-yielding bonds and time deposits. It is the savings banks which are suffering the most from this, loosing customers to both the commercial and co-operative banks. The savings banks are also handicapped by the way in which most of them are not allowed to give trade finance or investment advice, or to trade in securities.

The largest banks are reacting to the increasing competition by moving towards providing *Allfinanz* – an all-inclusive service of both corporate and personal finance – turning themselves into one-stop financial shops. On the retail side they are offering all the traditional banking services, together with mortgage finance, security dealing, life insurance and mutual funds. For corporate customers there are management consultancy services, real-estate services, equity funding products, venture capital, and mergers and acquisitions help and advice, as well as the normal corporate financing.

The Germans tend to invest heavily in insurance. Per capita spending on insurance is the highest in the Community, accounting for a third of all household savings, and making the market the richest in the EC (it is also one of the most protected). The market is very unconcentrated, with over 2,000 small, local companies. However, the largest insurance company (Allianz) does have 14 per cent of the life insurance market and 11 per cent of the non-life market. Insurance in Germany is expensive, because of the heavy regulation of the market. Both insurance rates and the wording of policies are strictly controlled, and individual insurance companies are not allowed to offer a complete range of policies to their customers. The banks are beginning to move into the market, linking up with insurance companies to sell policies through their branches, together with their own savings plans.

The mortgage market is not particularly open either. The main lenders of housing finance are the savings banks and specialized mortgage banks (*Bausparkassen*). The largest of the *Bausparkassen* are controlled by the major commercial banks. The mortgage banks are the only institutions allowed to issue mortgage bonds (which can be invested in by the insurance companies), which acts as a deterrent to newcomers entering the market. Loans (for as little as 60 per cent of the price of the house sometimes) can be obtained with the security of the mortgage bonds.

Credit card usage is low in Germany, with only about one adult in every 23 carrying credit cards. There are only 750,000 Visa cards and 700,000 American Express cards in circulation (compared with over 14 million Visa cards and 11.5 million Access cards in the UK), and they tend to be used more as charge cards than as credit cards. However, about a third of the population carry Eurocheque cards.

Together with the UK, Denmark and the Netherlands, Germany does not have any foreign exchange controls restricting the movement of capital. The financial markets are open and liberalized, and Germany acts as host to about 270 foreign banks, from 48 different countries, most of which are based in Frankfurt.

The dominant financial market is the bond market. In terms of the number of bonds issued, the market is the third largest in the world, behind New York and Tokyo. The main issuers are the banks, in particular the savings banks, and the government. In 1987, 80 per cent of the new issues volume was accounted for by just four banks – Deutsche Bank, Commerzbank, Dresdner Bank and Westdeutsche Landesbank. One of the reasons for the popularity of the market is the absence of any withholding tax on domestic bonds, unlike most of the other major bond markets. A 10 per cent withholding tax was briefly introduced in 1988, but the resulting outcry and flow of funds from the country persuaded the authorities to abandon the idea.

In contrast to the bond market, Germany's equity market is not particularly important. Most businesses raise the finance they need from the banks, rather than through share issues. Only 2,000 of the estimated 2 million companies in Germany have the equivalent of plc status, and only a quarter of these are quoted on a domestic stock exchange. Part of the problem is the fact that Germany has eight regional stock exchanges. The largest of them, at Frankfurt, has about two-thirds of the total market turnover, but there are still only about 30 shares regularly traded there. The existence of a stock exchange turnover tax of between 0.1 per cent and 0.25 per cent on all domestic secondary market trading does not encourage dealing either. This tax has also hindered the development of short-term securities, such as treasury bills.

In January 1990 a new market was unveiled. The Deutsche Terminborse (DTB) is an electronic screen-based options and financial futures trading system. At present the majority of deutschmark-denominated futures are traded on the LIFFE, which may suffer a loss of business as a result of this new market.

Greece

Greek banking can be summed up as over-concentrated, over-regulated, underdeveloped and uncompetitive. Three state-owned banks – the National Bank of Greece, the Agricultural Bank of Greece and the Commercial Bank of Greece – control about 80 per cent of the financial market. The remaining 20 per cent is divided between small, local, private banks and foreign institutions. The local banks are beginning to increase their share of the market at the expense of the foreign branches, by gradually improving their range of services and expertise. They are also noticeably more efficient and competitive than the state-owned giants.

A report in 1987 (produced by the Hellenic Banks' Association) identified two aspects in particular of over-regulation which posed great problems to Greek banks and handicapped their competitiveness. They were the way in which all interest rates were set by the monetary authorities, thereby effectively regulating the size of the banks' profits, and the large compulsory reserve requirements imposed on banks in order to finance the public sector deficit. Some steps have been taken to change this. The minimum rate for loans was abolished in January 1988, but the Central Bank of Greece still sets the interest rate for savings accounts (in 1988 it was 5 per cent), and agriculture and cottage-industries still receive subsidized rates on loans.

Bank reserve requirements were reduced as well, from 78 per cent of the banks' total deposits to 66 per cent. These requirements consist of a 7.5 per cent basic liquidity reserve, 10 per cent compulsory investment in small businesses, 10 per cent compulsory investment in public enterprises, and 38 per cent compulsory purchase of treasury bills.

Greece's capital markets are underdeveloped, with strict controls maintained over capital movements. Banks are companies' only source of investment capital. Reform is planned in this area, to develop effective markets and to abolish the present monopoly enjoyed by brokers.

Other markets which are underdeveloped include those of mortgage credit and insurance. The majority of house purchases are financed by money provided from outside the mortgage system, partly because of credit controls, while per capita insurance spending in Greece is the lowest in the EC. Both of these markets, like the banking system as a whole, are also very concentrated.

Ireland

Irish banking is concentrated, but there is considerable competition among the various financial institutions, with the different institutions overlapping in their provision of services. Eighty per cent of the banking market is controlled by the two major banking groups in the country: Allied Irish Bank and Bank of Ireland. The rest of the market comprises of two other small clearing banks: Irish National Bank (a subsidiary of National Australia) and Ulster Bank (a subsidiary of National Westminster Bank), together with public sector institutions (such as the Post Office Savings Bank) and another 20 foreign-owned banks. These are regulated in the same way as the domestic banks, but the majority of their business consists of providing foreign currency loans to companies.

A domestic market of only 3.5 million people means that competition between institutions is very fierce. Over the last few years the banks have been losing their share of the deposit market to building societies, life insurance and pension funds. In their turn the banks have been diversifying into mortgages and insurance provision: the Bank of Ireland first acquired its own building society in 1986, and it was the first bank to be given an assurance licence. The AIB has also diversified into these markets, and in 1987 set up its own stockbroking firm (AI Securities) as well. Both of these banks also have extensive branch networks in the UK and American subsidiaries, accounting for about half of their income.

The competition in the market has led to an increase in investment and services by the banks. For example, in 1987 the number of ATMs in Ireland rose to 77 per million people, compared with 35 per million West Germans and 30 per million Italians. The AIB is the first European bank to install 'script' ATMs at selected sites (such as supermarkets). These machines give customers valued paper, instead of cash, and are much less expensive to invest in than the normal ATMs. The AIB does share a normal on-line ATM network (with European compatability) too, with the Bank of Ireland and the Northern and Ulster banks.

Over half of the 67 insurance companies in Ireland are foreign owned, accounting for nearly 74 per cent of the total net insurance premiums paid in 1987. The Irish have a high household savings ratio (the average for 1980–7 was 17.8 per cent), and insurance spending is becoming increasingly popular. This is why the Irish market is so popular with foreign companies, despite the fact that they have to hold a greater percentage of domestic assets covering their liabilities than Irish insurance companies are required to (100 per cent, compared with 80 per cent).

The Irish securities markets are small and still fairly unsophisticated. The markets have developed since 1979, when the currency union with the UK was abandoned and sterling became a foreign currency, subject to exchange controls. They are dominated by government securities and have a rather limited role in providing business funds, and so

Irish companies are very dependent on bank borrowing for finance. There are several reasons for this, including the under-development of risk-management instruments, but the most telling is probably the tax system. This favours investments in government bonds (which are exempt from capital gains tax) at the expense of investments in private companies.

Although this market distortion remains, there have been major developments in the markets recently. For instance, to help increase market depth, institutions which are not members of the Stock Exchange are now allowed to buy more than 30 per cent of the equity capital of a brokerage company. Probably the most important development is the current establishment of an off-shore financial centre in Dublin – the International Financial Services Centre (IFSC). Institutions are to be encouraged to carry out foreign currency, futures and options dealing and fund and treasury management in non-Irish currencies in the IFSC through a range of incentives, such as exemption from local taxes and a corporation tax rate of 10 per cent (compared with the normal 43 per cent) for ten years. The IFSC will provide risk-hedging techniques, and will help the development and internationalization of Ireland's financial markets considerably.

Ireland still maintains some capital restrictions, mainly on short-term capital movements. However, restrictions between Ireland and other EC countries are due to be removed by the end of 1992, and restrictions between Ireland and non-EC countries will probably be lifted as well.

Italy

Italy's financial system is both concentrated and over-banked. There are just over 1,100 Italian banks, about 900 of which are small, rural savings or co-operative banks. The rest are almost all state owned, although there are some private commercial banks as well. However, just 16 of these 1,100 banks control 50 per cent of the deposit market.

Many of the small banks have been restricted to operating in certain areas only, while domestic entry to the market has been very controlled by the Central Bank: since 1966 only foreign institutions have been allowed to set up new banks in the country. The number of branches to receive authorization has also been limited; in 1986 only 500 branches, out of a requested 2,800, were allowed to be established.

As well as limitations on setting up and expansion, the banks are also restricted in the services they can offer, unlike the universal banks of some other EC countries. They cannot conduct merchant banking operations, or establish merchant banking companies, nor can they provide medium- and long-term funding, only short-term (up to 18 months). Longer-term funding has to be raised from special credit institutions. However, the banks can sell government debt instruments and mutual funds.

The Central Bank has been trying recently to ease the restrictions and supervision of the banks, and to promote competition among them, in order to allow them to become more efficient and to offer a wider range of services in the run-up to 1992. However, one of the factors which makes Italian banks uncompetitive internationally is their high costs, especially staff costs, and these show little sign of being reduced.

There is no formal mortgage credit sector in Italy. Instead, 71 per cent of house purchases are financed from personal savings. Variable rate loans can be obtained from the banks, but they are only short-term loans.

Credit cards are not popular among Italians, most preferring to pay for goods with cash. In 1985 a new card was introduced, the Carta Si. This was linked to 90 per cent of the banks, and carried agreements with both Visa and Mastercard. In spite of this, by 1987 only 800,000 Carta Si were in use, and they were acceptable in only 80,000 outlets. The Bancamericard of the Banca d'America & d'Italia is the most popular credit card in Italy, although it is linked only with Visa. However, the number of credit cards per capita is still very low compared with the majority of EC countries.

Expenditure on insurance is also low among the Italians in comparison with other member states. The life insurance market is very concentrated, with 63 per cent of it being controlled by the four largest insurance companies. The non-life insurance sector is, however, not so concentrated. There are restrictions on the investments that insurance companies can make, and so the returns from their business are low.

Italy is one of the countries in the Community which still

maintains some foreign exchange controls. These were eased in 1988, and were to be removed entirely by July 1990. Banks are now able to deal in futures, spot and forward foreign transactions, and currency swaps. They can now lend lira to non-residents and foreign currencies to Italians, and they can take unbalanced foreign exchange positions, up to 5 per cent of their foreign assets.

Luxembourg

Luxembourg acts as a unique centre of European financial activity, and is one of the most attractive financial markets in the world, although the Grand Duchy's authorities reject the idea that it is a tax haven. Its tax rules do make it appealing however: non-residents are not subject to withholding tax on either dividends or interest payments, there is no stamp duty, nor stock market transaction taxes, and corporation tax was only 34 per cent in 1989. Luxembourg also maintains customers' rights to bank secrecy in relation to the tax authorities.

Luxembourg does have other advantages as a financial centre, bar liberal tax laws. These include its location in the heart of continental Europe, and active official support for the financial sector and its growth. This support manifests itself in legislation on the sector and its regulatory system. For example, foreign institutions receive equal treatment with domestic ones, and there are no entry barriers against foreign banks setting up in Luxembourg (although there are minimum capital requirements which are much stricter than EC rules). There is also freedom of capital movement, and universal banking.

Because of a combination of these favourable factors and the extremely small size of the domestic market, very unusually international banking is of far greater importance in Luxembourg than the local sector. Of the 160 banks and savings institutions in the Grand Duchy at the end of August 1989, only 19 were from Luxembourg or Belgium (with whom Luxembourg has a special monetary association, allowing Belgian currency to be legal tender in the Duchy); of the rest, 65 per cent were from other European countries. Foreign currencies also accounted for 97 per cent of the institutions' total assets in 1987, and for nearly 86 per cent of their total liabilities.

The biggest area of business of the banks in Luxembourg is the Eurobond and other Euro-instrument markets. The banks account for 9 per cent of *all* Euromarket liabilities worldwide, and for 11 per cent of all Euromarket assets. Nearly 60 per cent of all public Eurobond issues are listed on the Luxembourg stock exchange, making up three-quarters of the securities quoted there.

There has recently been a slowdown in the Euromarket business, however, and, as a result, the banks have been diversifying their activities into such areas as treasury and pension fund management, foreign exchange dealing, trade finance and financial advisory services. One area into which nearly all the banks, both domestic and foreign, are expanding is the retail market. This had been rather neglected, especially by the foreign institutions, but now it is seen as a major growth prospect. The banks are competing to expand the range of services on offer, and the retail catchment area itself has been extended to include not just Luxembourg and Belgium, but also other neighbouring EC countries, such as France and West Germany.

Another important development has been the creation of open-end investment funds. These were introduced in 1983. By 1988 they accounted for over 40 per cent of the total net assets of Luxembourg's mutual funds, and contributed to the large increase in the number of such funds, from 76 in 1980 to 525 at the end of 1988.

The Netherlands

Together with the German, Danish and UK markets, Dutch banking is one of the most liberal and open systems in the EC. Deregulation of the industry and the abolition of foreign exchange controls have encouraged both competition and innovation within the market, and have led to more universal banking, with institutions offering a wide range of products and services to their customers.

The banking market is made up of commercial, savings and co-operative banks. The three largest banks (which include a co-operative, Rabobank) hold 71 per cent of the industry's assets, but there is still considerable competition, both between banks and between banks and other financial institutions, which are encroaching upon the banks' traditional territory. For example, investment fund companies are now challenging banks for the large market in savings: the Dutch have one of the highest ratios of savings to disposable income in Europe. The commercial banks have also been facing increased competition from the savings banks. These have been allowed to diversify into fund management, factoring, leasing, business lending and underwriting, although their previous tax advantages over the commercial banks have, in turn, been reduced.

Mortgage lending is another area where the banks have been competing more and more. Rabobank is the biggest single mortgage lender, but both the commercial and savings banks offer mortgages, as does the Postal Savings Bank. Traditionally, mortgage rates were fixed for a period of years, say five or ten, depending upon the maturity of the mortgage bonds issued. Now, however, variable rate loans have been introduced, together with bonds with very short renegotiating periods. Few mortgage bonds with a maturity of over seven years are now issued.

The Dutch insurance market is small and fairly concentrated, although many foreign companies and small domestic insurers do operate in it. Banks are prevented from writing insurance risks, although they can link up with insurance companies and sell life assurance with mortgages. The Netherlands is only one of three member states where independent insurance intermediaries are allowed to operate, and the market in general is one of the least regulated in Europe, with no government control of insurance rates or policy wording.

Portugal

Portugal has probably the least sophisticated and developed financial sector in the EC. Despite tremendous efforts to develop the banking system and to increase the efficiency of the financial markets since the mid-1980s, a great deal still has to be done.

Before the reforms the financial sector was dominated by overstaffed, undercapitalized, inefficient state-owned banks – commercial, deposit and investment ones. These banks controlled almost all retail market savings (99 per cent of retail savings were held in the form of bank deposits in 1984) and corporate borrowing, because of the lack of capital markets offering alternative methods of saving and borrowing. The sector was also heavily regulated, with credit ceilings, strict foreign exchange controls (there was not even a foreign exchange market; all transactions had to be conducted through the Central Bank), and restrictions on interest rates.

However, things have been changing. Competition has been developed by the opening up of the banking market to foreign institutions and private domestic banks. These new private banks have won a share of the market by trying to provide the same services and professionalism as the foreign banks, in conjunction with their knowledge of the local market. Competition has been increased between the banks and specialized credit institutions as well. Commercial and investment banks are now permitted to give medium-term mortgage loans, while the credit institutions can now take medium-term deposits (over one year) from households.

The state banks are being reorganized. In July 1989 the fourth largest nationalized commercial bank (Banco Totta & Acores) had 49 per cent of its shares floated, and the largest state bank (Banco Português do Atlântico) is due to be privatized in 1990.

The large insurance market has also been opened up to private companies and foreign insurance firms, and independent investment and pension funds have been encouraged too.

Major developments have been carried out in the capital markets, so that 23 per cent of corporate finance was raised on them in 1987, compared with almost none in 1984. The number of institutions quoted on the Portuguese Stock Exchange has also risen from 1985's level of 50 companies, to 192 in 1988.

In 1977 an interbank money market was set up, and a year later an interbank securities market. They were designed to encourage investment in medium- to long-term debt instruments, in order to reduce the excess liquidity that the financial system was suffering from at the time. An important step occurred in 1985, when short-term marketable treasury bills were introduced. These provided households with an alternative method of saving to bank deposits, and gave banks a new investment instrument. Other securities were introduced in 1987, offering higher yields and longer maturities, such as marketable five-year certificates of deposit. Equity certificates (which do not confer ownership) have also helped private companies to raise capital on the markets.

In other moves, credit ceilings have been removed, and interest rates have been derestricted. However, foreign exchange controls are still in place, although banks are now allowed to trade spot foreign exchange balances with each other (but they can only hold working balances of foreign currencies). Anomalies still exist in the system which restrict free market forces; for example, treasury bonds are tax free, but CDs are subject to a 15 per cent withholding tax.

Spain

The financial market in Spain is extremely overbanked and very regulated and inefficient, despite attempts by the government to improve matters. There are 350 banks and savings banks, with a total of 16,500 branches between them. This amounts to one branch per 2,300 Spaniards (compared with a ratio of 1:3,800 in Britain, 1:5,500 in France, and 1:9,900 in Germany). The largest six commercial banks control about 75 per cent of the market, but are still fairly small when compared with the major EC banks. In order to increase the banks' competitiveness, and to protect them against foreign predators in the run-up to 1992, the government is encouraging them to merge. The biggest commercial bank was formed by the merger of two of the seven largest banks, Banco de Bilbao and Banco de Vizcaya.

The commercial banks are notoriously inefficient: it is estimated that they are overstaffed by about 30,000 people. They offer only a limited range of services (markets such as house finance, pensions and life assurance are very underdeveloped), and as late as February 1988 bank staff voted against extending banking hours into the afternoon.

In the past there has been little incentive for the banks to improve their efficiency. They faced little competition from either the savings banks, which were restricted to operating only in their home areas, or from foreign banks, which are allowed to set up only three branches each in the country (unless they take over a local branch network), and so are limited to providing wholesale finance only. There was also little competition between the commercial banks, partly because of the Spaniards' habit of placing their accounts with the branch nearest their home rather than shopping around the different banks. However, this is now beginning to change. The savings banks, in particular, are challenging the commercial banks. These are now allowed to merge and so expand into new areas, they are not overstaffed, and they offer a range of retail services, especially to small and medium-sized companies. The larger savings banks are even diversifying into areas such as leasing.

The banking system does suffer from government restrictions, which reduce competitiveness, although some are now being removed. The banks are obliged to buy low-interest-yielding government securities, and for every Pta 100 they keep on deposit they have to place Pta 29.5 either in the Bank of Spain or in treasury bills, to help finance the government. In 1988 there was also a minimum reserve requirement of 19.5 per cent.

One area in which there has been reform is the stock market. A single automated market with continuous trading has replaced the previous system of ten-minute sessions of open outcry. A single price is also now quoted for shares traded on the Madrid, Bilbao, Barcelona and Valencia markets. An automated bookkeeping system has been introduced, in order to speed-up the settlement process, and the stockbrokers' fixed commissions and monopoly over transactions are to be ended. Since 1990 Spanish banks and companies, and those from other EC countries, are able to own up to 30 per cent of a brokerage company. From 1992 these institutions will be able to become members of the Exchange themselves (provided they meet certain conditions, such as capital requirements). However, restrictions on the permitted volatility of share prices still remain, and share prices are still quoted as a percentage of their nominal value, rather than in pesetas.

Despite its problems, or, rather, because of them, the Spanish banking sector is seen, especially by foreign financial institutions, to present tremendous opportunities. The interest margins in the retail sector are very high, the highest in the Community, producing a 1 per cent return on assets. Non-banking services, such as insurance, mortgages and pension funds, are undeveloped and are major future growth areas. These factors make the market extremely attractive to both foreign institutions and to those domestic banks which can exploit their rivals' weaknesses, as the savings banks are doing.

Comparison of the different systems

As can be seen, the 12 existing banking systems in the Community vary considerably in their development, sophistication, openness and operations. The most developed and competitive are the systems of Germany, Denmark, the Netherlands and the UK. These are the countries where universal banking is practised, where exchange controls are not enforced, and where the least government regulations and restrictions are imposed. The markets of France, Italy, Belgium and Ireland suffer some restrictions still, and the respective governments still maintain some exchange controls, preventing the full development and internationalization of the markets. Spain, Greece and Portugal have the least competitive and sophisticated banking systems, and suffer the most from over-regulation and inefficiency.

However, it is a characteristic of all the Community markets that in the last few years, in the run-up to 1992, there have been tremendous efforts to modernize, improve, strengthen and open up the financial sectors, in order to allow each country's institutions to compete most effectively when the single European market comes into operation.

The players

The top 50 European banks in terms of capital are shown in Appendix I, together with the EC banks in the European top 300 by country. The largest banks are those of France, Germany, Italy and the UK, with ten, nine, seven and seven banks respectively in the top 50. The only other EC countries represented in the top 50 are Belgium, Denmark, Spain and the Netherlands.

THE IMPORTANCE OF FINANCIAL SERVICES TO THE EC ECONOMY

The financial services industry is of growing importance to the EC's economy. All companies have to use financial services, and so the efficiency of the financial institutions and markets has a crucial 'knock-on' effect on that of all the other industries.

In 1985 the Cecchini Report (see pp. 90–106) tried to make a quantitative assessment of the importance of the financial services industry to the economies of the eight major member states, and to that of the Community as a whole, by examining data on employment, value added, and output.

The report discovered that the financial services sector (encompassing banking, finance and insurance) employed over 3.1 million people in the Community (rising 23 per cent between 1978 and 1985), over 3 per cent of the total workforce. The percentage for each country was normally between 3 per cent and 4 per cent of the workforce, although for Luxembourg the figure was 7.7 per cent. Germany, France and the UK accounted for 70 per cent of this total employment. The insurance sectors consistently employed fewer people than the banking and finance sectors.

In terms of value added, 6.7 per cent of the Community's total gross domestic product in 1985 was contributed by the credit and insurance sector. Luxembourg had the highest contribution, with 14 per cent, with the lowest contribution in France, at 4.5 per cent. Table 1.1 details the results. Bank loans were used as a measure of output for the banking sectors, in order to calculate output as a percentage of gross domestic product for each country. Table 1.2 shows the results.

These figures show how the financial services industry is of great importance to the EC as a whole, and to both the UK and Luxembourg in particular.

INTRA-EC BANKING ACTIVITY

As was mentioned in the analyses of the individual EC banking systems, most of the other member states are not as open to foreign banks as the UK is. Because of this, British banks have had their activities on the Continent limited, and they have a very small share of the EC market. At the end of

Table 1.1 Value added in credit and insurance, 1985

Country	ECU M	% GNP
Belgium	5,966	5.9
Germany	44,417	5.5
Spain	13,929	6.1
France	29,277	4.5
Italy	26,998	5.6
Luxembourg*	535	14.0
Netherlands	8,537	5.4
UK	70,240	12.6
Total	199,899	6.7

Note: * 1982 figures.

Table 1.2 Bank loans outstanding as percentage of GNP

Country	Bank loans
Belgium	142
	(1982 data)
Germany	139
Spain	99
France	93
	(1986 data)
Italy	96
Luxembourg	6,916
Netherlands	130
UK	208

1987 less than a quarter of British banks' external claims were on EC countries, compared with about half of the UK's export of goods. The total claims of UK-registered banks on EC countries was only £51 billion, and of these the majority (72 per cent) were to other banks: 19 per cent of the loans were to private-sector non-banks, and the balance was to public-sector bodies.

This lack of openness in cross-border banking can be illustrated by a comparison of the number of other EC bank branches and subsidiaries that can be found in three of the major Community banking countries: France, West Germany and the UK. Table 1.3 shows the numbers and origins of the different EC banks in each country.

It should be remembered that these figures do not include banks' representative offices in other countries (which do not generally undertake banking business), and they do not take into account the relative attractions of each of the host countries for foreign banks.

Table 1.3 EC branches and subsidiaries, 1988

Home country	France	West Germany	Britain
Belgium	1	1	6
Denmark	0	2	6
France	–	6	18
West Germany	5	–	17
Greece	1	1	1
Ireland	0	0	1
Italy	7	5	15
Luxembourg	4	2	3
The Netherlands	3	5	8
Portugal	4	0	3
Spain	6	3	7
Britain	10	7	–

Chapter 2

The European Community and the single market programme

BACKGROUND TO THE EUROPEAN COMMUNITY

The development of the European Community

The European Community (EC) is not actually one community, but three, each one established by a separate treaty. The communities are:

1. *The European Coal and Steel Community* (ECSC), set up by the ECSC Treaty signed in Paris in 1951. Its aim was to lock the coal and steel resources of the participating countries irrevocably together, so that they could never go to war against each other again.
2. *The European Economic Community* (EEC), set up by the Treaty of Rome in 1957. Under this treaty the principles of the ECSC were extended and the Common Market was established. The purpose of this was to combine the national markets of the member states into one community, by allowing the free movement of goods, services, capital and workers between the states, and establishing community-wide policies on such matters as agriculture, transport and competition.
3. *The European Atomic Energy Community* (Euratom), set up by the Euratom Treaty, signed in Rome at the same time as the EEC Treaty. This treaty's aim was to establish the safe development of nuclear energy for peaceful purposes.

No formal merger of these three communities has taken place, but, although they each cover different areas, they do have several basic similarities. They were established by the same member states, they have the same fundamental objectives, and they share the same institutions. Therefore, in 1978 the European Parliament adopted a Resolution that they should be known collectively as 'The European Community'.

Originally there were six member states of the three communities: Belgium, West Germany, France, Italy, Luxembourg and the Netherlands. In 1973 Denmark, the Irish Republic, and the UK joined them, and in 1981 Greece became a member of the EC. In 1986 the number of member states rose to 12, with the additions of Spain and Portugal. The combined population of these countries is over 320 million, giving the EC a total population far in excess of either that of the United States or Japan.

The institutions of the European Community

The Community has four main institutions, each with a different role in the EC's administration and decision-making process. They are the Commission, the Council, the European Parliament, and the Court of Justice.

The Commission

The Commission is made up of 17 members, two each from France, West Germany, Italy, Spain, and the UK (which are the five largest member states), and one each from the other EC countries. The commissioners are appointed every four years, and each one is responsible for a certain area (or areas) of Community policy. They are also each responsible for at least one of the Commission's 22 directorate generals.

All Community action starts with the Commission, as it submits all proposals and drafts for Community rules to the Council. The Commission is also responsible for carrying out the decisions made by the Council, and for supervising the day-to-day implementation of the Community's policies. The Commission also has to make sure that the treaties' provisions and Community measures are implemented properly (in its role as 'Guardian of the Treaties'), and it can take action against those member states which do not comply with EC rules.

The Council

The Council is made up of representatives of the various governments of the member states. This term 'Council' is normally used to refer to the Council of Ministers, although it can also include working groups of officials from the different countries. The Council of Ministers is the Community's most powerful body by far, and is its decision-making institution. The Council has the last word on all Community legislation, and it is where the conflicting interests of the different member states and the Community as a whole are reconciled.

The Council considers all the proposals put to it by the Commission, and can either adopt them as they stand, ask the Commission to amend them, amend them itself, reject them totally, or take no decision on them at all. If the Council is unable to reach an agreement on a measure, then the proposal can be passed up to the European Council (or the 'Summit'), made up of the presidents and prime ministers of the states.

There are 76 votes available in the Council, weighted so that the larger member states have more influence than the smaller ones. The four biggest countries have ten votes each, while Luxembourg has only two votes. Decisions are taken by unanimity, by a simple majority, or by a qualified majority (at least 54 votes). This system of weighted votes means that it is possible for the smaller states to outvote the large ones, which, unlike the smaller countries, would be more able to withstand any political pressure designed to bring them into line.

The European Parliament

The European Parliament is the only Community institution which is directly elected. It has 518 members (81 from the UK) who make up political parties, instead of being merely representatives of the member states. The members are elected every five years, the last election being in June 1989.

The main powers of the Parliament are concentrated on the setting of the Community's budget. It has an 'advisory and supervisory' role in connection with Community legislation;

its formal opinion is needed on many proposals before the Council can adopt them. Parliament's role in this area was extended by the Single European Act of 1987. Under this a two-reading 'co-operation procedure' was set up. Parliament now reads and gives its opinion on any suggested legislation, and may suggest amendments after the Council has formed a view on it (or come to a 'common position'), as well as when the proposals are first made by the Commission.

The Court of Justice

The Court of Justice comprises 13 judges, (including one from each of the member states), assisted by six advocates general. They are responsible for ruling on the interpretation and application of Community laws. Such a Community court is essential for the uniform application of EC laws, because otherwise they could be interpreted and enforced differently in each state.

The Treaty of Rome established the Court of Justice because of the new ideas about competition and fair trade implicit in the Common Market proposals. Most of the actions reaching the Court are concerned with breaches of these rules. Actions can be brought to the Court by governments, local authorities, companies and individuals, if they feel that the Community rules are not working fairly. If the Community rules are actually being broken, the Commission can invoke the power of the Court to see that they are enforced. Companies which break Community law can be fined by the Court; governments cannot be. However, in the past the Court has found that the moral pressure it exerts has been enough to make erring governments comply with the laws.

Other bodies

In addition to the four constitutional institutions discussed above, the treaties provided for three auxiliary institutions. These are:

1 *The Economic and Social Committee*, a body made up of 156 representatives from a range of groups, including manufacturers, businessmen, employees, the self-employed, farmers, trade unions and consumers. The committee

advises the Council and Commission on economic and social matters, and so has a strong influence on the Community's decision-making process.
2 *The Court of Auditors*, consisting of 12 members appointed by the Council. It audits the Community's income and expenditure to make sure its financial management has been sound.
3 *The European Investment Bank* (EIB), the Community's financing agency. The EIB provides loans and guarantees for capital investment projects. These help the balanced growth of the EC and often promote investment in less-developed regions in order to create new jobs. Sometimes the investment is for projects of common interest to several member states.

Community legislation

There are three types of Community legislation. *Regulations* are directly applicable to all member states and their citizens. If there is any conflict with existing national law, these regulations take precedence. *Directives* are also binding on all member states in connection with the results which are to be achieved and the time by which they are to be achieved. However, the means by which the results are achieved are left to the individual national governments. Directives do not have any legal force in the member states, but if they are not implemented particular provisions may take a direct effect on the country concerned. *Decisions* are legally binding, but only on the particular governments, companies, or individuals to whom they are addressed.

There are also two types of legislation which are not legally binding but which merely state the views of the institution which issues them. These are *recommendations* and *opinions*.

The legislative process is very complex, and usually rather lengthy, as it involves much consultation and negotiation between the different institutions. The following is a simplified summary. The Commission submits proposals to the Council, which reaches agreement on them, often after consulting with the Parliament and the Economic and Social Committee. This 'common position' is submitted to the Parliament, which can approve, amend or reject it. The

Council, however, has the final authority, and it may choose to go against the Parliament's decision, although only by unanimous agreement.

Several changes in the legislative process were made by the Single European Act (SEA), which came into force on 1 July 1987. The most important change, in relation to the internal market, was the extension of the use of majority voting in the Council on single market proposals. Now there are only a few specific issues on which unanimity is required. (These are taxation issues, the free movement of people, and the rights and interests of employees.) Unanimous voting requirements often held up decision making, and so this measure has speeded things up considerably.

THE 'COMMON' MARKET?

The idea of creating a single, 'common' market in the Community originates in the 1957 Treaty of Rome. The opening lines of the Treaty laid down this goal:

> The Community shall have as its task, by establishing a common market and progressively approximating the economic policies of member states, to promote throughout the Community a harmonious development of economic activities, a continuous and balanced expansion, an increase in stability, an accelerated raising of the standard of living and closer relations between the States belonging to it.

The Treaty set out specific provisions for the free movement of goods, services, capital and people in order to achieve the single, integrated European market envisaged in it. However, the progress towards creating this common market has been extremely slow. Tariffs and quota restrictions on goods between member states were removed by 1968, but the momentum was not sustained and, since then, little was achieved. The vision of a true common market with no barriers to internal trade and no distortions in competition has not been realized. Many old, non-tariff restrictions remain, and some new ones have been set up too.

Two factors have contributed to this lack of progress. First, the Community has widened its activities to include matters such as regional policy, research and development, and environmental considerations. These, together with the admission of six new member states to the Community, have taken attention away from the development of the Common Market. Second, and probably more important, has been the attitudes of the governments of the individual states. They all want the benefits that a true common market will bring, but have often not wanted to make compromises that would have an adverse effect on their own countries. This reluctance was especially strong in the 1970s and early 1980s, when a world recession followed the quadrupling of Middle Eastern oil prices. The high inflation, structural unemployment and low growth of this period meant that governments preferred to follow protectionist policies rather than support a common market. These attitudes helped expose the weaknesses inherent in the Community's decision-making process, as unanimity was still required on most common market proposals. Progress towards a single market eventually came to a standstill because of these protectionist policies and unanimous voting requirements, and in the early 1980s intra-Community trade ceased to grow altogether relative to extra-Community trade.

THE SINGLE MARKET PROGRAMME

By the beginning of the 1980s it was obvious that the Community's competitive position in the world was getting worse. In the advanced high-technology industries it was falling behind both the USA and Japan, and newly industrialized countries like Taiwan and South Korea were capturing markets in traditional industrial goods. At the same time there was a growing awareness among the national governments (and in the UK in particular) that the benefits for each member state which would ensue from a truly integrated EC market would be far greater than the disadvantages that could arise from isolated aspects of such a market.

This awareness led to the setting up of a study group by the Commission to consider how the Community could achieve its economic potential. This resulted in the publishing of a White Paper ('Completing the internal market') in 1985, drafted by the commissioner with responsibility for the internal market, Lord Cockfield.

The 1985 White Paper

The 1985 White Paper is the most comprehensive and far-reaching attempt yet to fulfil the vision of a common market within the Community. Unlike previous attempts, this White Paper tries to identify and remove *all* the existing barriers to the free functioning of the market, instead of concentrating on one economic sector or on minor changes easily acceptable to every member state. It puts forward over 300 legislative proposals to remove existing barriers and regulations. This blanket approach is vital, because, as many of the barriers interact, unless they are all removed the principle of the single market could be badly undermined.

The date for the completion of the programme was chosen as 31 December 1992. It was not intended that the barriers should all be removed on that particular day. Instead, the date is meant to mark the end of the programme, with all the restrictions being lifted by then. A detailed timetable was set out in the White Paper for implementing the package of proposals between 1985 and 1992. It provided for most of the Community legislation needed, to be adopted in the earlier years, with the last two years being used by individual governments to enact and implement the required national legislation.

Removing the barriers

The White Paper deals with three categories of existing barriers which prevent the free movement of goods, services, people and capital: physical, technical and fiscal barriers.

Physical barriers

The divisions between the Community's member states are at their most obvious at Europe's internal frontiers. Customs checks and immigration controls often cause long delays in the movement of both goods and people through Europe. These controls on goods also impose additional costs on companies which carry out cross-border trade (through transport and handling charges), thus reducing their competitiveness. The majority of frontier controls on goods are because of different national technical standards and different levels of indirect taxation in the member states. These differences have to be removed before the physical frontier controls can be lifted. This illustrates why the comprehensive approach towards the common market adopted by the White Paper is needed. The Paper contains detailed measures designed to eliminate or greatly reduce these differences.

Frontier controls are also needed to protect countries from terrorists and drug smugglers, to detect illegal immigrants, and to enforce health standards. A Europe without any internal frontiers is not possible until alternative ways of dealing with these matters have been found. Common approaches to the drug and terrorist problems will have to be adopted (already there is close police co-operation on these matters in Europe), external frontiers will have to be tightened, and the Community will have to agree on a common policy on the movement of third-country citizens between member states.

Until such common policies have been implemented the Community can only simplify and speed up internal frontier checks and crossings. Proposals have been made to reduce checks on people by only stopping them on exit from a member state (not on both entry and exit), and only if there is a reason to do so, instead of systematically as at present. Fast entry channels for EC citizens are proposed at major European crossing points, and the introduction of European passports will further help.

To help cut down on delays through controls on goods, the 'Single Administrative Document' was introduced on 1 January 1988. This replaced about 100 forms which used to be used throughout the EC for despatch, transit and entry formalities, and which made a simple lorry journey from, say, the UK to Germany via a Dutch port a costly and time-consuming administrative nightmare. The next stage towards removing all controls on goods will be the co-ordination of national agricultural, taxation, health, and transport policies, so that all the controls will be able to be removed by 1992.

Technical barriers

The elimination of physical barriers has to be paralleled by the elimination of technical barriers. These differences in standards and regulations which create technical barriers help prevent free trade in goods, and can also affect people.

Different national product regulations and standards mean that many goods have to be altered, or even manufactured separately, so that they can be sold in different European markets. The manufacturer, therefore, has to incur very much higher R & D and marketing costs, as well as increased production costs due to losing any available economies of scale. Although the product standards set by each country are normally to protect the health and safety of its citizens and their environment, such standards can be used as a form of protectionism. When this occurs one country will refuse to allow certain goods of another country to be imported simply because they are not exactly the same as its own goods, or it will not recognize another country's health and safety tests on goods and so still insists that the goods have to meet its standards as well.

Previous attempts by the Community to get rid of these technical barriers were not very successful. The Commission tried to get governments to change their national regulations and standards so that they all conformed to agreed EC standards. This proved to be a very complex, long and difficult process. The White Paper's approach is different. Instead of trying to harmonize the diverse regulations so that all states' goods meet the same standards, the Paper proposes that minimum standards for health and safety should be agreed upon, and that a product can be designed and manufactured in whatever way a company wants, provided that it meets these minimum standards. This approach will mean that consumers will still have maximum choice, and that the member states will (it is hoped) find it much easier to agree on proposals.

Barriers to the free provision of services are included under the heading of 'technical barriers' in the White Paper. Services have an important role in the economy of the Community, and have become as important as manufacturing in their contribution to European employment. However, there has been far less progress towards eliminating barriers restricting the provision of services than there has been for goods. The White Paper's approach is similar to the one it uses for goods: mutual recognition of other countries' standards, backed up with minimum common rules where it is felt that these are necessary, rather than the total harmonization of regulations.

The services industries covered in the Paper include new ones, such as information technology, as well as the traditional industries like banking and insurance.

Technical barriers may restrict people directly too. The non-recognition of educational and training qualifications gained in different states can prevent individuals from getting jobs in other Community countries. The Commission proposes that there should be mutual recognition of academic and vocational training qualifications and of professional qualifications (provided that minimum requirements for qualifications, training and experience are met).

Fiscal barriers

One important function of frontier controls is to allow the member states to collect the excise duties and VAT on goods to which it is entitled. Borders between Community countries can only be abolished if and when new ways are found to deal with these tax payments. This is the reason why the Commission has been trying to harmonize indirect taxes in the Community for over 20 years (since the first VAT directive of 1967). But, however, the structure of excise duties and the VAT rates and coverage still vary widely between states.

Under the present system, VAT accrues to the country where the goods are finally consumed, as VAT is relieved on exported goods and imposed on imported goods. Under the system proposed by the Commission, VAT would be charged on intra-Community trade in the same way as it is on purely domestic trade now, with exporters charging the same positive VAT rate on exported sales as for domestic sales, and with importers reclaiming this rate as input VAT in the same way as they would for domestic purchases. Displaced revenues would be reallocated to the correct countries through a clearing mechanism, such as banks, airlines and railways already in use, with the balances being settled at intervals (either daily, weekly, or monthly). A similar system has also been proposed for collecting excise duties levied on goods.

However, problems arise because of the different rates of VAT and duties charged by different countries. Without any frontier controls these differences would lead to distortions in trade, as people in highly taxed countries would simply cross over the border into a lower taxed country to shop because of the much lower prices (the popularity of the current duty-free allowances point to the potential for this!). To prevent this distortion in trade, the Commission proposes approximating the various VAT rates of the member states. They do not intend that the rates should be identical throughout the Community, but that they should be near enough each other so that there is not sufficient incentive for people to shop abroad for tax reasons. Two common VAT bands have been suggested: a lower band of 4–9 per cent, for goods which are socially sensitive, and an upper band of 14–20 per cent for other goods. In addition, the Commission has suggested the complete harmonization of excise duties.

There has been a lot of opposition to these ideas to remove fiscal barriers. For example, it has been suggested that the VAT clearing house system and the method of collecting excise duties could be even more trouble for businesses than the current systems are. However, the strongest opposition has been directed at the proposals for approximating VAT rates. The UK government has led this opposition, as the measures would mean abandoning zero VAT rating on some goods (such as children's shoes and clothes, books and cold food). Britain has argued that it is not necessary to approximate VAT rates, as market forces would do this automatically if the divergence in rates did distort trade – those countries which lost trade because of their high VAT rates would lower their rates. It would be necessary to set only minimum VAT rates, it argues, to prevent competitive tax cutting. It is felt by some UK bankers that if any tax rates are to be harmonized they should be those of corporation and withholding taxes, because variations in these distort where producers rather than purchasers will locate. So far there has been no agreement on the approximation of VAT rates, but a transitional system of payment (by which traders pay the rates charged in the country of the goods' destination) has been agreed upon by the Council.

Fiscal barriers are proving to be the hardest to break down, and are provoking the most argument and controversy. The governments of the member states are very reluctant to allow the Community to make any changes in their tax systems as such changes (and, in fact, any changes in fiscal matters) are often interpreted as threats to the states' national sovereignty. Progress is further hampered by the unanimous voting requirements attached to taxation measures. Because agreement has been so difficult to reach, some of the fiscal proposals in the White Paper have been dropped, and more may be in the future.

The progress of the Single Market Programme

The single market programme has made substantial progress since 1985, although perhaps not as much as the Commission had hoped for. The third annual progress report on the programme (published by the Commission in March 1988) showed that 208 of the programme's proposals had been presented to the Council, but only 69 of these had been adopted (and most of these were only relatively minor measures). Progress had fallen behind that laid out in the White Paper's timetable, and was very uneven – almost none had been made in some areas (such as the free movement of individuals), and there were considerable problems in others (e.g. the plant and animal health sector). However, proposals which were not originally in the White Paper are being incorporated into the single market programme whenever a new need is identified; for example, proposals for a free market in the telecommunications industry have been added. Many of these extra proposals have been adopted.

The changes in the decision-making process which the Single European Act introduced in 1987 have had the overall effect of speeding up the programme. Initially the SEA did cause a backlog of work, with the introduction of the two-reading co-operation procedure with the European Parliament, but this was more than compensated for in the latter stages of the legislative process, with qualified majority voting being used for most decisions in the Council. By January 1989, 109 of the remaining 279 proposals in the programme had been adopted, 121 were awaiting adoption, and only 49 were still waiting to be tabled by the Commission.

The SEA affirmed the Community's commitment to completing the internal market by 31 December 1992. It defined the single market as 'an area without internal frontiers in which the free movement of goods, services, persons and capital is ensured in accordance with the provisions of this Treaty'. The ratifying of the SEA by the Parliaments of all the member states also confirmed each country's commitment to the 1992 programme. At the Hanover Council in June 1988 four areas were given priority for future progress by the heads of government of the states. These were the areas of intellectual property, public procurement, common technical standards, and banking and financial services.

Public awareness in the UK of the single market programme and its significance was initially very low. In the autumn of 1987, surveys showed that only 5 per cent of British businesses appreciated what the programme was about and the importance of the 1992 date, compared with 79 per cent of French businesses. These figures led the Confederation of British Industry and the Department of Trade and Industry under Lord Young to start the campaign 'Europe Open for Business'. This was designed to promote 1992 and its challenges and opportunites to British businesses. The campaign was remarkably successful: a year later the proportion of UK businesses aware of 1992's significance had risen to 90 per cent.

The UK is very dependent upon trade with the rest of the Community, and so it is vital that businesses are ready to take advantage of the opening up of the European markets. Figure 2.1 shows how the pattern of Britain's international trade has shifted away from the traditional market of the Commonwealth to the EC market since the UK joined the Community. By the end of 1989 the EC accounted for over half of both the UK's total exports and its total imports, compared with about 35 per cent of both total imports and exports in 1972. It is likely that, after 1992, trade with non-EC countries will decline even more.

The external trade position

It is feared by many non-EC countries that the internal market will form a 'Fortress Europe' – a protectionist Community market from which they are excluded. The Community's position is that access to the EC market for companies from non-EC countries should be based on reciprocity, or how EC companies are treated in those third countries. This idea of reciprocal treatment has caused a great deal of concern among

The EC and the single market programme 41

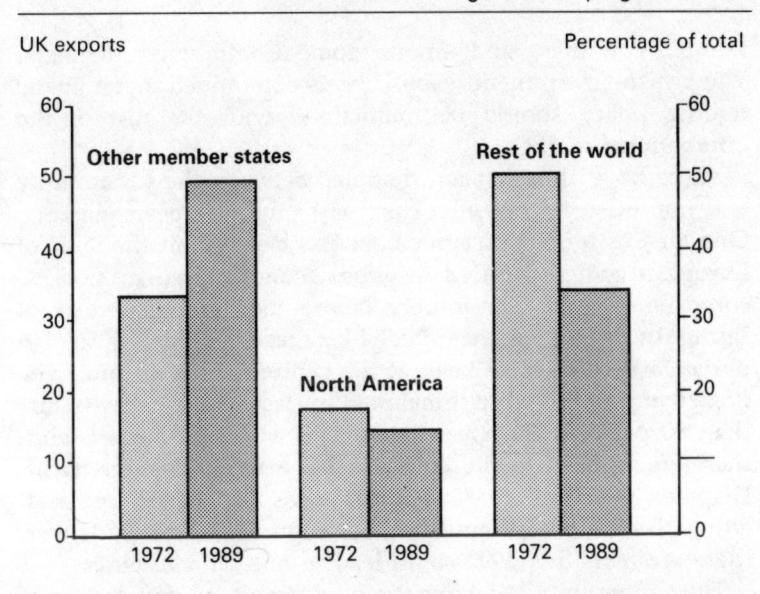

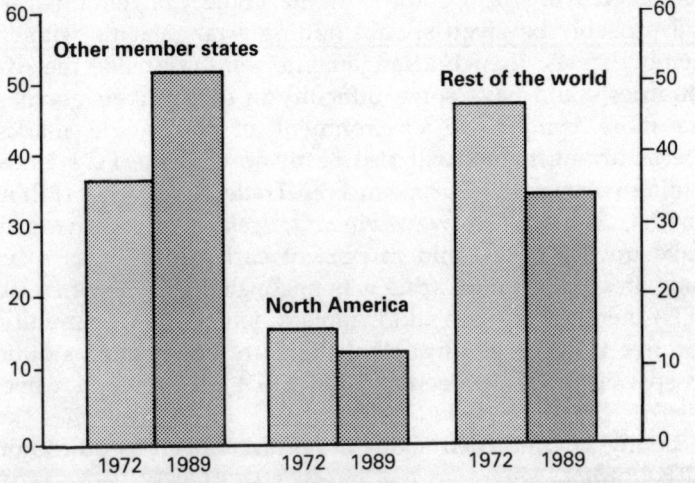

Figure 2.1 UK trade patterns, 1972–89*

Note: * Figures for 1989 January–November only.
Sources: *Economic Progress Report* 198, October 1988; *Business Monitor, Overseas Trade Statistics of the UK*, November 1989

non-EC countries, and among some Community members. The British government, especially, is determined that a liberal trading policy should be maintained with the rest of the international market.

There have already been disputes between the Community and non-EC countries about access to the European markets. One area of serious disagreement has been about the level of European content needed in goods manufactured by non-EC companies in the Community before they are classed as of European origin. It has been Japanese products (cars in particular) which have been at the centre of this dispute. The French authorities have threatened to classify any car with less than 80 per cent European content as a foreign import, and, therefore, subject to the common EC external customs tariff. Disputes over imported US meat have also flared up, and, although both the EC and the USA want to avoid a trade war, there are fears that 1992 could lead to one with America.

The Community is taking steps to make sure that certain of its trading partners will still have access to the new market. The African, Caribbean and Pacific (ACP) countries (many of which are former British and French colonies) are already associated with the EC through the Lome Conventions, and will probably be given special trading arrangements with the member states. If such arrangements were not made the ACP countries could have some difficulty in selling their goods in the more competitive environment of the single market. Special arrangements will also be made with the EC's largest trading partner, the European Free Trade Association (EFTA). Austria, Sweden, Norway, Finland, Iceland and Switzerland make up the EFTA, and at present each country has a free trade area with the EC (this was negotiated in 1973 when two EFTA members, Britain and Denmark, joined the Community). The free trade areas mean that there are only customs duties on special goods between EC and EFTA countries. However, despite the intended arrangements, EFTA countries are becoming as concerned about EC protectionism as other non-EC countries.

The external trade policy of the EC will be shaped by its obligations under the General Agreement on Tariffs and Trade (GATT), as well as by its own decisions. GATT agreements mean that countries are forbidden to discriminate against the trade of other GATT signatories, and are not permitted to increase any trade barriers without giving corresponding concessions in return. The Community's position on external trade was set out by the 1988 European Council meeting in Hanover, when it was confirmed that the Community intended to remain open to non-EC goods, subject to reciprocal treatment for Community goods. The Council concluded that

> The internal market should not close in on itself. In conformity with the provisions of GATT, the Community should be open to third countries, and must negotiate with those countries where necessary to ensure access to their markets for Community exports.

The economic implications of 1992

Substantial economic benefits are expected to be created by the improvements in resource allocation brought about by the removal of market barriers. The starting point in this process is the removal of non-tariff barriers within the EC, and it is expected that this will begin a chain of events with both micro- and macro-economic consequences. The main microeconomic effect will be a reduction in costs, caused directly by the removal of physical and technical barriers, such as frontier controls and differing product standards. However, it is argued that the increased competition throughout the Community will produce gains which are far more substantial than just this cost reduction.

Economists maintain that this unrestricted competition will generate a continuous downward pressure on prices, particularly in those markets which currently are protected. These lower prices will encourage demand and allow companies to increase their output. This increased output will, in turn, enable companies to take advantage of economies of scale and so reduce costs even more, making them even more competitive internationally.

The consumer will benefit the most from all this, as price differences between the member states will be greatly reduced and overall prices of goods will be lowered. Consumers will have greater choice, as well as cheaper goods, as more competition will lead to new companies and products entering the market and to increased innovation from existing businesses. However, all this competition and downward pressure on prices will cause problems for companies, as profit margins may initially be reduced by more than they are increased by lower costs. This will mean that companies may suffer a net decrease in their profits. The companies hardest hit by this profit decrease will be those which have been enjoying protected markets or monopolies. However, the economies of scale, increased sales and lower costs are expected to more than make up for these reduced profits when the firm is competitive. The overall effect will, therefore, be a gain in the Community's net economic position and the creation of more efficient companies better able to compete effectively in the world market.

Market integration will also lead to wider macro-economic effects on the main economic indicators of the Community – inflation, unemployment, public budgets, Gross Domestic Product and the external trade position. The general regeneration of the EC's economy, together with the lower prices caused by open public procurement, will ease member states' public deficits. The price reductions which should occur throughout the economy should mean that the Community's economic growth is not accompanied by increased inflation. In turn, this inflation-free growth should reduce unemployment levels. Finally, the external trade position of the Community should be improved by businesses' increased competitiveness.

The above benefits may not occur immediately, however. For instance, unemployment levels may rise, not fall, initially because increased productivity will probably be gained through reductions in the costs of the factors of production, i.e. through reductions in labour and capital. It is in the medium term that these job losses will be more than made up for by the growth in demand, and so growth in output. These benefits are obviously important in themselves, but they could lead to still greater gains. As they represent the relaxation of four major economic constraints, these benefits should allow authorities more opportunities to follow policies which will lead to even greater improvements in the economy.

In his book *The European Challenge 1992* (a summary of an extensive report for the Commission), Paolo Cecchini tried to quantify the potential benefits from market integration. He used a variety of approaches, both macro- and microeconomic, and estimated that the overall medium-term gains will be 4–9 per cent of total EC GDP. There are a number of methodological problems in the research (see pp. 103–4), but, even after allowing for a broad margin of error, it is clear that the single market programme should provide the Community with major economic gains.

Cecchini emphasized that governments, businesses and the Community have to act appropriately in order to realize the programme's full economic potential. Governments have to enact agreed Community proposals rapidly, so that the 1992 programme is given credibility. If governments are seen to be half-hearted about the internal market, businesses are unlikely to prepare and benefit from it. Businesses have to become efficient and competitive. Competition is not going to increase only between EC companies, but also between EC and non-EC firms operating in the enlarged market. Unless EC companies meet the challenges presented to them, the main beneficiaries from the single market could be non-EC companies and countries. For its part, the Community has to maintain a credible competition policy. Without this, lower costs might not be passed on to consumers through lower prices, and so the increase in demand might not materialize. If this increase does not happen the single market will merely produce larger profits for businesses.

Chapter 3

The current position and the Commission's approach

PROGRESS BEFORE THE WHITE PAPER

The right of establishment and the freedom to provide services throughout the Community were specifically laid out in the Treaty of Rome's directions for the internal market. However, far more progress was made in dismantling barriers to trade within the EC than was made in removing barriers to the free provision of services. Progress in derestricting financial services throughout the Community was especially slow, despite the fact that the financial sector is of considerable importance to the EC economy, accounting for 3 per cent of the total employment in the Community and for about 6.7 per cent of its total GDP, as was shown on p. 24. Although financial services are becoming more and more global in nature, the factors which are responsible for this (such as financial innovation, competition, deregulation and new technology) are not of a specifically European nature.

Progress towards an integrated financial market before the 1985 White Paper was very limited. The First Banking Co-ordination Directive of 1977 set out the minimum legal requirements credit institutions had to meet in order to be authorized in member states: namely, to have adequate capital and to be directed by at least two people of good repute and experience. If a credit institution met these requirements a basic right of establishment was created, allowing banks which had their head offices in one member state to set up branches in other member states. The principles of home country control were also introduced. This directive was a useful first step, but the basic right of establishment does not create a free internal market. For instance, there has to be freedom to provide financial services on a cross-border basis too.

There was one other measure which concerned banking before the White Paper was commissioned. This was the 1983 Directive on Consolidated Supervision. This laid down that where one institution owned more than 25 per cent of another the two should be supervised together, on a consolidated basis. The home authorities would thus be able to get a global view of the group's activities. Although helpful, this directive did not represent the removal of any major barrier to business.

Therefore, many obstacles to the free provision of financial services still remain. This is shown by the wide variations in price between financial products in different member states. The prices of products in some countries are consistently either higher or lower than the Community average, while other countries are comparatively expensive for some services and inexpensive for others. The most expensive member states are Italy and Spain, and this can in part be explained by the fact that they are also the countries which retain the most barriers to foreign competition in financial services in the EC. These price differences are examined in detail on pp. 99–101.

The lack of progress in cross-border trading in the Community has meant that banking (and retail banking especially) has remained very much a national business. Institutions are able to earn far greater profits in their domestic markets than they can in foreign ones, and so they tend to concentrate their operations in their home countries.

THE EXISTING REGULATORY BARRIERS

Barriers to banking in general

The provision of financial services is not affected by physical barriers, nor by many fiscal barriers like VAT rates and excise duties, although it may be by other fiscal considerations, such as differences in withholding tax rates. However, technical barriers do have a great impact on financial services. Just as there are different national technical standards for goods, so are there different standards of supervision and regulation for financial institutions and services in the different member states.

There are two aspects to a free EC market in banking: establishing a local presence in the various member states and providing services across frontiers. The situation as regards barriers to these operations is very different, although some obstacles do have an effect on both activities.

The term 'establishing a local presence' can refer to the establishment of branches, representative offices or subsidiaries. However, when 'freedom of establishment' is mentioned it is normally in connection with the freedom of banks to set up branches in other member states. For there are very few problems associated with setting up a representative office abroad – often the bank does not even need permission from the authorities – and when a subsidiary is set up foreign banks are subject to the same requirements and regulations as domestic banks, with no discriminatory barriers. (The setting up of a subsidiary abroad, however, does not really represent the provision of services by an institution in another member state, as subsidiaries are separate legal entities from their parent institutions and are usually classed as banks of the countries in which they are set up.)

As was said above, a basic right of establishment for financial institutions was created by the First Banking Co-ordination Directive. In essence, this right means that the entry and establishment rules for foreign banks are the same as for domestic institutions in each member state. Therefore banks from one EC country are able to compete on equal terms with the domestic banks in another Community country, provided that their branches are set up in accordance with the host country's national requirements and that they obtain authorization from the relevant authorities in each member state in which they wish to establish a local branch. As a result of this directive there are now very few overtly discriminatory regulations.

However, the way in which institutions have to obtain

authorization from each member state in which they want to set up branches, and the way that these branches then come under the control and supervision of the host countries, are great obstacles to the free establishment of branches in other member states. To obtain authorization, the branches have to meet the host country's requirements on such things as minimum capital and solvency ratios, which differ from state to state. This acts both to make certain Community countries less attractive than others to institutions (because their requirements are stricter), and to discourage the setting up of branches at all, as obtaining authorization is often costly and time-consuming.

One of the biggest barriers to the free establishment of branches throughout the Community is that, with the exception of the UK, all the member states require foreign branches to comply with domestic minimum capital regulations and to maintain their own endowment capital (or 'own funds'). This means that, in effect, branches are treated as separate banks, even though their creditors are creditors of the bank as a whole, and not just of that branch. The UK is the only Community country to recognize that this is inappropriate, although it does require that foreign branches maintain adequate liquidity levels and keep within agreed foreign currency exposure guidelines. This 'own funds' requirement represents a major impediment to branching, especially if a bank wishes to set up branches in a number of member states, because it means that large amounts of capital have to be tied up quite unnecessarily. An added complication is that the definition of a branch's capital varies from state to state!

In some countries a 'comfort letter' is required before a branch can be set up. This is a guarantee of support from either the parent bank or from the domestic supervisory authorities. The importance of such a letter varies – some countries do not require one at all, while in Italy restrictions are placed on the branch's activities if it is not provided – but its provision is not seen as a very onerous obligation. Other barriers to the establishment of branches sometimes also exist. For example, there may be restrictions on the legal form banks may adopt; in Belgium the branch's parent institution has to be a commercial company. There may also be limits on the number of branches that can be set up; in Spain, for instance, the maximum number of branches a foreign bank can establish is three.

As far as the provision of cross-border services is concerned, the main direct barrier to this is the existence of exchange controls. Exchange controls are a major obstacle, and their removal was one of the four fundamental aims of the Treaty of Rome when it envisaged a single market. They are discussed in detail on pp. 51–4.

A bank still faces restrictions on its activities, regardless of whether it establishes a local presence in another member state or provides cross-border services. This is because the operations of foreign banks are subject to host country supervision and regulation, and so are limited to those activities which domestic institutions are allowed to carry out. This host country regulation is not much of a problem where the domestic market is deregulated, but is a major barrier when the market is a very restricted one. The opposite problem occurs in West Germany. There a banking licence will only be given to institutions which provide a full range of banking services, and so banks from countries which have fragmented banking markets might not receive authorization. Host country supervision also means that the authorities may restrict the way in which branches can conduct their business, and require them to meet certain prudential standards (for example, for solvency ratios and large exposures). Again, these supervisory regulations differ between the member states.

Barriers to the securities business

In addition to these barriers to general banking there are also some barriers which specifically affect the securities market. These have an impact on banks' activities because often they are important players in the securities business. The main barrier is the fact that some EC countries do not allow foreign banks to become members of their stock exchanges, either by not allowing foreigners to become licensed stockbrokers, or by separating commercial banking and broking and limiting the legal right to trade on the exchanges to brokers. The impact of these restrictions on stock exchange membership and trading rights depends upon the structure of a particular country's securities market. In Italy, for example, domestic bonds and shares can be traded directly between banks without going through the exchanges, and so the ban on stock exchange membership does not prevent foreign banks from dealing in securities. In France, however, all securities have to be traded on the exchanges.

Even in those countries where foreign institutions are allowed access to the exchanges there may be some minor restrictions on their activities. Often foreign banks are not allowed to lead manage any domestic stock issues. Sometimes there are also regulations preventing or limiting the purchase of foreign securities; in Spain there is a limit on the number of foreign securities that banks can hold in their portfolios. There may also be discriminatory taxes on the purchase of foreign securities, which tend to discourage foreign banks from trading in those markets, as less restricted markets are more attractive.

EXCHANGE CONTROLS

One of the most important barriers to the free provision of financial services throughout the Community is the existence of exchange controls, and their removal is a prerequisite for an integrated financial market. The securities market is most affected by the presence of exchange controls, where they represent the most important barrier to a free market in that industry. Exchange controls also affect the cross-border provision of services, as they may stop foreign banks taking deposits from a country's residents, or from lending to them. Therefore all exchange controls have to be abolished before a single market in financial services can be set up.

The Treaty of Rome laid down the free movement of capital as one of the essential conditions of an internal market, together with the free movement of goods, services and people. Exchange controls have been abolished by some member states, but this has been the result of decisions by national governments, and not because of any EC legislation. In 1962 the Community decided that member states had to allow the free movement of capital for direct investment. But there was no further progress towards removing the many other exchange controls still in existence in most member states before the 1985 White Paper.

However, after the White Paper was published the Commission introduced a two-stage process designed to remove all exchange controls by 1992. Stage one was agreed at the end of 1986, when a directive was adopted to liberalize formally certain cross-border transactions. These transactions included those in unlisted securities, bond issues, unit trusts and long-term trade credits. The directive came into effect on 1 March 1987 for the majority of member states. Greece, however, was given until the end of 1988 to implement it, and Spain and Portugal have to put it into effect between 1989 and 1992.

The second stage consisted of a directive, adopted in June 1988, removing all the remaining controls on capital movements, including those affecting bank accounts, financial loans and short-term monetary instruments. Most countries have to comply with it by July 1990, although Spain, Portugal, Greece and Ireland were given until the end of 1992 to do so. However, because of the difficulties the directive could cause those countries with less developed financial markets, Greece and Portugal have been able to negotiate longer transitional periods, and now have until 1995 to remove all their exchange controls. Therefore, there will not be full freedom of capital movement in the Community until 1995, slightly later than first planned. The progress made in this area since the White Paper has been considerable, however; the majority of member states' exchange controls will be abolished by 1992.

As well as the deferred implementation dates the directive contains other provisions to help ease the transition for countries with less-developed financial markets. It allows for a fund to be set up to help those member states which get into financial difficulties because of the removal of exchange controls, and it also contains a safeguard clause. This clause permits countries which experience severe balance of payment difficulties to re-impose exchange controls, although only temporarily. The Commission would have to give the country permission to take this step (except in an emergency), and the clause only refers to those controls on short-term operations which are removed by the directive.

The fund which the directive establishes combines two

existing facilities, and would provide medium-term financial assistance to member states experiencing balance of payments difficulties. If this happened, loans of up to 16 billion ECU (about £10.5 billion) could be made, normally financed by market borrowing. A final clause of the directive includes a statement of intent to liberalize capital movements between the Community and non-EC countries, thus looking forward to the global deregulation of financial markets.

The extent to which exchange controls are currently imposed by the member states varies greatly, and there is quite substantial financial provision between EC countries already. All exchange controls in the UK were abolished in 1979, and full freedom of capital movement also exists in Denmark, West Germany and the Netherlands. Luxembourg and Belgium have controls only to maintain their dual exchange rate system (which separates current and capital account transactions), and have agreed to phase this out by the end of 1992. But there are extensive exchange controls in Spain, especially in the securities market (for example, restricting the buying and selling of foreign securities), and French residents are not allowed to hold foreign bank accounts or foreign currency accounts in France, and there are restrictions on the number of French francs banks can lend to non-residents. In Italy there are restrictions on loans by residents to non-residents and on foreign borrowings too, although many of the controls which used to exist have been abolished.

Exchange controls tend, in general, to limit capital outflows from a country, rather than capital inflows. Because of this, and the fact that the UK does not have any exchange controls, the capital transactions of UK residents are subject to fairly few restrictions, and so the removal of exchange controls by the other member states will not have much effect on them. There will probably not be any sudden large outflows of capital in 1992, with UK residents transferring their money to other member states, as they have been free to do so since 1979. Therefore UK banks are unlikely to be too affected by losses of deposits to other EC banks providing cross-border services in the UK. However, the removal of exchange controls will give opportunities to UK banks to provide cross-border services to residents of those countries which still maintain controls, and which will be far more affected by their abolition than the UK will be. For example, French residents will be able to open bank accounts in the UK, and Greeks will be free to borrow from UK banks without needing authorization.

NON-REGULATORY BARRIERS

The barriers mentioned above are all official barriers, imposed by legislation and regulation. As well as these there are a number of unofficial (and often unavoidable) barriers to foreign banks operating in other member states. Probably the biggest unofficial obstacle to a financial institution doing business in another country is the cost of entering the market. This is normally very high, especially for retail banking, where a large branch network is needed to gain access to the small retail account deposits which are the lifeblood of the market. The costs involved in establishing such a network, whether it is by buying branches or by building them, are phenomenal. Although these costs do not discriminate directly against foreign banks (as domestic institutions have to incur them as well), they are a significant disincentive, as the foreign institutions will normally have already paid out large sums to set up one network in their domestic market. Domestic banks also have an advantage over foreign ones when it comes to assessing the risks and opportunities of the market, as they possess detailed local knowledge and expertise.

Other unofficial barriers which are very hard to overcome are ones associated with national culture and preferences. Financial services are provided in many different ways in the different Community countries, as was shown in Chapter 1. To take just one example, depending on which member state they are in house buyers can obtain mortgage finance of between 70 and 100 per cent of the property price, at either fixed or variable rates of interest, from either a specialized mortgage bank, or a savings bank or a normal commercial bank. However, in some countries the buyers would pay for their house out of their own savings, with perhaps just a short-term bank loan to help them out. Such customs are not likely to change because a foreign bank offers a different product. Most people tend to stick with what is familiar and well known, especially where banks are concerned, and this will make it difficult for foreign banks to gain a substantial market share in other member states even when all the official restrictions are removed.

THE COMMISSION'S APPROACH

The Commission's goal is to create a totally integrated European financial market by 1992, with full freedom of establishment and freedom to provide cross-border services. To do this it has proposed a series of interacting measures which will allow financial institutions to operate across the Community without needing separate authorization from each member state, and which at the same time will provide savers and borrowers with adequate protection.

The Commission's approach to financial services is the same as that underlying the 1985 White Paper, and therefore the entire single market programme. It is based on three fundamental, interdependent and complementary concepts: minimum essential harmonization, mutual recognition and home country control. Each one is essential to obtain the overall goal of a single financial market in the Community.

The early approach of the Commission was to try to achieve the complete harmonization of all national standards and regulations. This turned out to be impossible, because the huge differences in national standards meant that in most cases no agreement could be reached, and where agreement was possible it was an extremely long process. Instead, the principle of mutual recognition was adopted. The idea of this is that the financial supervisory authorities of each member state recognize the way in which the authorities in all the other member states supervise and regulate their financial institutions.

Mutual recognition will only be accepted and put into practice, however, if it is accompanied by the implementation of a minimum essential level of harmonization of prudential standards, to protect investors and borrowers. This minimum set level of standards is necessary because without it market forces would reduce the minimum standards of each country to those of the member state with the most relaxed system of banking supervision. The Commission does *not* intend this to happen. 'Minimum harmonization' means setting sufficient minimum regulations to ensure borrowers and savers are protected and to safeguard the stability of the financial system. It does not mean reducing supervisory standards to the level of the lowest common denominator. The standards set may be higher than those currently in force in some Community countries and lower than those of others, but that is not a primary consideration.

With the elements of mutual recognition and minimum essential harmonization in place, the principle of home country control can be applied. Under this the activities of financial institutions throughout the Community, regardless of whether they are carried out by providing cross-border services or by branches in other countries, are supervised by the authorities of the member state in which the institution is based, although the authorities of the host country will still be responsible for some aspects of regulation.

Using this approach of basic home country control, backed by mutual recognition and minimum essential harmonization, to formulate its legislation, the Commission aims to remove all the remaining barriers to a free banking market in Europe by 1992.

THE LEGISLATIVE PROGRAMME

The most important Community measure on the operation of EC-based banks is the Second Banking Co-ordination Directive. This is supported by four other measures, which establish certain aspects of the minimum harmonization needed, and which are essential for the Banking Directive's effective implementation. These are:

1. A directive on the own funds of credit institutions;
2. A directive on a solvency ratio for credit institutions;
3. A recommendation on deposit protection schemes;
4. A recommendation on the monitoring and control of large exposures.

Other measures which affect credit institutions are:

1. A directive on the reorganization and winding-up of credit institutions;
2. A directive on the annual accounts of banks;
3. A directive on the accounts of foreign branches.

All of these measures are discussed in the next chapter. There are also directives on the liberalization of capital movements, which will have a great effect on banking operations.

Chapter 4
The legislative measures

THE SECOND BANKING CO-ORDINATION DIRECTIVE

The Second Banking Co-ordination Directive is the centrepiece of the Commission's programme for an internal market in banking, and it is by far the most important piece of Community legislation on the removal of barriers to the free provision of banking services yet to be proposed. The Commission issued the Directive on 13 January 1988, and it was finally adopted on 18 December 1989. Its provisions are to be implemented by the member states over the three years to 1 January 1993.

The Directive plugs a number of gaps left by the First Banking Co-ordination Directive of 1977, and, together with two parallel directives on solvency ratios and the own funds of institutions, forms a comprehensive framework for regulating all the Community's banking business. The Second Directive applies to all credit institutions in the EC, except those which were specifically excluded by the First Banking Directive. The First Directive defined a credit institution as 'an undertaking whose business is to receive deposits of repayable funds from the public and to grant credits for its own account'. Those institutions which the Directive excluded from this definition are:

1 National central banks;
2 Post office giro institutions; and
3 Certain other institutions specific to each member state.

(In the UK these include municipal banks, credit unions, and the National Savings Bank.)

Table 4.1 Scope of the Second Banking Directive

1. Deposit-taking and other forms of borrowing
2. Lending (consumer credit, mortgages, factoring, trade finance)
3. Financial leasing
4. Money transmission services
5. Issuing and administrating means of payment (credit cards, travellers cheques, and bankers drafts)
6. Guarantees and commitments
7. Trading for own account or for account of customers in:
    (i) money market instruments (cheques, bills, CDs, etc)
    (ii) foreign exchange
    (iii) financial futures and options
    (iv) exchange and interest rate instruments
    (v) securities
8. Participation in share issues and the provision of services related to such issues
9. Money broking
10. Portfolio management and advice
11. Safekeeping of securities
12. Credit reference services
13. Safe custody

Source: Second Banking Co-ordination Directive

The single licence

The most important aspect of the Second Directive is the provision for a 'single banking licence'. This will allow any credit institution which is authorized to act as such in a member state automatically to set up branches, or to supply cross-border services, in all the other member states, without having to obtain further authorization from each state. An appendix to the Directive lists a wide range of services for which this licence will be valid. Table 4.1 shows this list. A bank will be able to provide any of the services on the list in all the other member states, provided that it is authorized to do so in its home country. It will be able to provide these services, even if the host country does not allow its domestic credit institutions to provide them.

This feature of institutions being able to provide services regardless of whether or not the host country banks can is important. In those countries which persist in maintaining tight restrictions on the range of activities their banks can carry out, domestic institutions will find themselves at a disadvantage compared to institutions based in countries without such restrictions, such as the UK. It is expected that this situation will prompt widespread deregulation in the more restricted countries; although member states are not obliged to remove any restrictions on the operations of their domestic banks by the Directive, countries are unlikely to maintain regulations which discriminate against their own credit institutions. However, it has to be said that until this deregulation takes place, institutions based in markets which are already liberalized (such as Britain and Germany) will have a great advantage, because they can provide the whole range of banking services. (In theory, British banks can undertake any activity they wish, provided it is not illegal, although, in practice, the Bank of England may object if it does not consider it to be prudent.)

The list of activities shown in Table 4.1 is very wide-ranging, taking account of the realities of the financial markets and the gradual breaking down of the traditional demarcations between commercial and investment banking. What is especially important is that the list includes all forms of securities transactions. This will have a huge impact on those countries which still keep their commercial banking and securities business separate. To take account of future developments in banking services the Directive provides for the periodic review and up-dating of the list. Licensed institutions are even allowed to provide services not included in the list in other member states, if the host country gives them permission to do so.

The scope of the single licence

The single banking licence only applies to credit institutions which are authorized as such by their home authorities. This concept of mutual recognition does not extend to institutions which do not have this authorization, even if their business is included in the Directive's list of recognized activities and if they are allowed to provide these services in their home countries.

The Second Directive does, however, extend mutual recognition to non-credit financial institutions which are subsidiaries of authorized credit institutions, although they have to meet certain strict conditions. The Directive covers such institutions because, in some member states, credit institutions are not authorized to undertake some of the recognized activities directly, but have to provide them through subsidiary companies. Such activities include leasing, factoring, securities dealing and mortgage credit provision. The subsidiary has to fulfil the following conditions:

> Its activities have to be fully consolidated with those of its parent credit institution;
> The parent institution has to own at least 90 per cent of the subsidiary's shares; and
> The parent institution has to accept full responsibility for the subsidiary.

Endowment capital

The other major way in which the Second Banking Directive helps to remove barriers to banking throughout the Community is by abolishing the requirement for branches to maintain a minimum level of endowment capital. As was said in Chapter 3, branch minimum endowment capital rules are a very large obstacle to the free establishment of branches in other countries, because of the huge, unnecessary costs they impose on banks. The Directive provides for these minimum capital levels to be totally removed by 1992, and for a transition period before then, during which the maximum level of branch endowment capital which can be demanded is 50 per cent of that needed for domestic credit institutions to be authorized.

Minimum harmonization

Although increased competition among credit institutions should bring substantial benefits, unlimited competition could be a destabilizing influence on the financial system. The application of the principle of home country control could also encourage institutions to base their businesses in the member state with the lowest standards of supervision in the

Community. In order to prevent these things happening, the Directive includes provisions to harmonize some essential supervisory standards: those concerning minimum capital, the control of major shareholders and bank participation in the non-bank sector.

Minimum capital

At present, the level of minimum capital that a credit institution needs to maintain varies considerably between the member states. Under the Directive, a credit institution will have to have a minimum initial capital level of 5 million ECU in order to obtain authorization. If they wish, member states will still be free to apply a higher level of minimum capital to their domestic institutions. However, it is unlikely that any state would apply a higher level because, in effect, it would be discriminating against its own institutions.

This 5 million ECU minimum capital level does not just apply when an institution is seeking authorization, but it has to be maintained on a continuing basis. An institution's funds are not permitted to fall below this level during the entire time it is conducting its business. Those credit institutions which were authorized before the Second Directive comes into force have until the end of 1996 to meet this minimum capital requirement.

Control of major shareholders

Banking authorities have to have the power to supervise the ownership and control of credit institutions by organizations/individuals with non-banking interests, in order to prevent cross-financing and the conflicts of interest which can happen in complex group structures. According to the Directive, the supervisory authorities have to be informed of the identities of an institution's major shareholders together with the size of their holdings when it applies for a banking licence. The authorities then have the power to refuse to authorize a bank which has a group structure which they consider to be inappropriate.

As with the minimum capital requirement, this control over the major shareholders of an institution is to be applied on an on-going basis. The institution has to inform the authorities annually about the identity and interests of its major shareholders, and any investor who is considering acquiring a major stake in a credit institution, or full control over one, has to inform the authorities first so that they can examine the acquisition and, if necessary, refuse to allow it. This double information obligation should mean that any group structure that the banking authorities consider to be 'detrimental to safe and sound banking management' will not be allowed.

Bank participation in the non-financial sector

Supervision of bank participations in the non-financial sector is considered necessary to ensure the financial stability and soundness of the banks. This is partly because of contagion risk – a bank's soundness could be affected if a subsidiary in which it had a major equity stake got into financial difficulties. It is also necessary because any equity stake in another organization constitutes a long-term freezing of the bank's assets. Again, the present rules governing bank participations vary widely across the Community countries. The Directive aims to impose some harmonization in this area by setting two prudential limits:

1 No participation in any one non-credit or non-financial business should exceed 10 per cent of a credit institution's own funds;
2 The total value of a credit institution's participations in such undertakings should not exceed 50 per cent of its own funds.

Certain steps which supervisory authorities can take to ensure compliance with these provisions are also suggested in the Directive.

Home and host country control

The principle of home country control features very strongly in the Second Directive. The banking authorities of the home countries will have responsibility for most aspects of supervision, including the application and monitoring of those minimum standards of harmonization mentioned in the last section, together with ensuring that there are good administrative, accounting and internal control mechanisms in place in foreign institutions' branches under their supervision. However, host countries will have the primary responsibility for supervising liquidity, and exclusive responsibility for implementing monetary policy. In order to make these tasks easier, the Directive states that, if they are asked to do so, branches established in other member states should give the host authorities the same amount of information as that required from the country's domestic institutions for monitoring liquidity and controlling monetary policy.

The host country authorities will also have the power to supervise banking solvency in relation to the securities business. They will be able to apply measures to control the level of market risk which is assumed by foreign banks trading in their domestic markets. (Market risk reflects changes in interest or exchange rates; in contrast, credit risk is the risk that loans will not be repaid, and is covered by the Solvency Ratio Directive.) This provision will mean that there will still be an obstacle in the way of banks undertaking new securities business, which are already adequately capitalized under their home country's standards. The UK's Financial Services Act contains such a distinction between overall bank solvency and solvency in relation to securities business, and the separation was introduced into the Directive to take account of this Act.

Host country rules on the way in which banking services are provided and business is conducted are also to apply. However, these rules cannot be used to discriminate against foreign institutions, and have to be 'justified on the grounds of the public good' (although just what constitutes 'the public good' is not stated!).

Co-operation between competent authorities

The Second Banking Directive greatly strengthens co-operation between the banking authorities of the different member states. The home country authorities are given the right to undertake on-the-spot checks of their domestic banks' branches in other countries, after first informing the host authorities. At the same time, the authorities in the host countries also still retain their rights to check branches established in their states.

Another clause in the Directive lays down specific rules in order to increase the harmonization of professional secrecy binding on all banking authorities in the Community. The rules apply specifically to the exchange of information between member states' authorities, and to employees and ex-employees of the authorities.

There are detailed provisions in the Directive for co-operation between the authorities before branches are established in other EC countries. The home country authorities will first assess the viability of the proposals and the adequacy of the institution's structure, and only after they are satisfied about these will they give the information to the prospective host authorities, and therefore give permission for the branch to be set up. Where the provision of cross-border services is concerned, notification of intent by the bank is sufficient for the home country authorities. The Directive does also provide for a consultation procedure between different national authorities when an institution proposes to set up a subsidiary in a different member state.

All the rules governing the supervision of credit institutions in the Directive are enforceable, and the member states are obliged to impose adequate sanctions for any infringements of them.

Reciprocity

The part of the Directive which has attracted the most attention and controversy is its proposals on reciprocal access to the single market for institutions from non-EC countries. Originally these amounted to third-country banks only being allowed access to the internal market if banks from the Community enjoyed similar freedom in the third countries' home countries. Under the present situation, subsidiaries of third-country banks established in the EC are considered to be Community undertakings, and, therefore, will benefit from the Directive's provisions for freedom of establishment and cross-border banking. It was argued by the Commission that, as the EC was about to become one of the most open banking markets in the world, in a highly financially interdependent world Community banks should be allowed fair access and equivalent treatment in the other world markets. It felt that the

Directive's reciprocity arrangements would ensure this fair treatment for EC banks.

The Directive first proposed that when a non-EC bank's subsidiary requested authorization to set up business in a member state the supervisory authorities in the country concerned were to suspend their decision until the Commission had investigated the matter. This involved the Commission checking on whether the banks of all the member states received reciprocal treatment from the third country in question. If they did not, then authorization was to be suspended until negotiations with the country ensured such reciprocity. The investigations were to be carried out on a case-by-case basis by the Commission, as they arose, and could take up to three months. The process was also to apply when a non-EC bank proposed to buy a stake in a Community bank.

These proposals provoked a tremendous amount of opposition, both within the EC and from third countries. The UK, Germany, Luxembourg and the Netherlands were all against the provisions, fearing that, instead of resulting in better treatment for EC banks, they would merely mean that non-EC banks would be denied access to the European market. The UK's concern was that this could have an effect on London's position as an international financial centre. It was argued that non-EC banks in Europe would help to keep prices competitive and ensure that the costs of banking services were not maintained at artificially high levels by EC-wide cartels. What was even worse, it was felt that the reciprocity rovisions could have actually led to reduced, rather than increased, access for Community banks in third countries, as non-EC countries took protectionist measures in retaliation. In fact, the US Federal Reserve Board threatened to do this.

Because of the strength of feeling against these reciprocity provisions, the Commission did eventually change them. The demand for reciprocal treatment has been toned down into one either for national treatment (i.e. EC banks in a third country should receive the same treatment as that country's domestic institutions), or for effective market access, comparable to that which the third country's banks receive in the Community market. Cases are no longer to be considered individually. The Commission will now draw up a report periodically (the first one six months before the Second Directive comes into operation) on the treatment EC institutions are receiving in third countries concerning the provision of services and the acquisition of holdings in non-EC banks. In those countries where EC banks do not receive effective market access or national treatment the Commission will propose negotiations with the countries' authorities to get fairer treatment. Where Community institutions do receive national treatment in non-EC countries, the authorities in the member states do not have to inform the Commission of any requests for authorization from banks of those countries; they can simply allow them to set up business. Where EC banks do not receive national treatment the Commission can suspend the authorization of new institutions from the country concerned for up to three months while negotiations take place. However, this suspension does not apply to institutions from the country which are already authorized in a member state. They can expand into other states just like all other authorized EC institutions.

Criticisms of the Second Banking Directive

The Directive has been criticized on a number of grounds, apart from on its original reciprocity proposals. It will not succeed in removing all the regulatory barriers to a free market in banking services, although it will go a long way towards establishing an open market and reducing the present bureaucracy. For instance, the host country will still be able to impose a three-month delay before a branch can be set up, in addition to a possible three-month delay before the home authorities approve of the proposal and inform the host country authorities. One month's notice also has to be given before a branch can offer a new service, and, as has been said, a bank has to give notice to its home authorities before it offers cross-border services.

Criticism has been made of some of the prudential standards in the Directive, on the grounds that they are too onerous. The British Banking Association (BBA) took this view (although generally welcoming the Directive and its overall effect), especially regarding the continuous application of the minimum capital requirement. The 5 million ECU minimum level is more than three times that required at present in the UK, being equivalent to approximately £3.5 million. The BBA also thought that the controls on bank participations in non-financial institutions were too strict.

The Banking Directive will leave some barriers still in place, in the form of the remaining aspects of host country supervision, especially those of conduct of business rules. These rules are generally imposed to safeguard consumers, and their extent varies between the member states. In the UK such rules include the Consumer Credit Act and the Financial Services Act. (While other Community institutions will not need to be authorized under the latter to carry out investment business, they will have to comply with its conduct of business regulations – unless they can prove them not to be 'justified on the grounds of the public good' to the European Court of Justice.) Nor does the Directive remove the barriers preventing foreign banks becoming members of some countries' stock exchanges, or stop some member states from requiring all securities business to be conducted on their stock exchanges. The Commission is, however, expected to act on these issues before 1992.

CAPITAL ADEQUACY MEASURES

In itself, the Second Banking Directive cannot ensure that banks are adequately capitalized to protect depositors, and therefore it is linked to two complementary measures which do deal with this. These measures are the Own Funds and Solvency Ratio directives. A final provision in the Banking Directive states that the concepts of mutual recognition and home country control contained in it can only come into effect if these two directives are implemented at the same time.

The directives apply to the same credit institutions as the Banking Directive does, and form a vital part of the harmonization of prudential standards needed to complete the internal banking market. There are two reasons for this. First, capital adequacy is crucial to protect investors and depositors, and for the stability of the whole banking system. Recently, capital ratios have been gradually eroded, which makes it all the more important to strengthen them now for the single market. Second, these ratios, and the methods used to calculate them, have to be harmonized to ensure fair competition after 1992.

The Own Funds Directive

The Own Funds Directive was proposed by the Commission in September 1986 and was finally adopted in May 1989. Its purpose is to amalgamate the wide variety of national definitions of an institution's 'own funds', and so to improve the comparability of the prudential ratios of Community banks. The 'own funds' of banks are often referred to in Community measures for banking co-ordination. They are especially important in measuring the solvency of institutions, as they form the numerator of the solvency ratio. However, banks' own funds have never really been defined, apart from very vaguely in the First Banking Co-ordination Directive. This Own Funds Directive provides a precise, harmonized description of the term, which will allow banking authorities to know that supervisory standards are basically equivalent throughout the Community.

The definition includes all the elements which currently make up institutions' own funds in the different member states, and uses a two-tier classification by dividing them into 'internal' and 'external' elements. 'Internal elements' (which are also called 'tier 1 capital') are those which are at the bank's free disposal, and which can absorb any losses. There are five main sub-groups of these internal elements:

1 Paid-up capital and share premium account, but excluding the institution's holding of its own shares;
2 Reserves, including legal reserves and accumulated retained profits;
3 Revaluation reserves;
4 Funds which are at the bank's free disposal in order to cover normal business risks, where there is evidence of their existence in the internal accounts and where their amount is determined by the management, verified by independent auditors, and made known to the competent supervisory authorities; and
5 Securities of indeterminate duration, and other similar instruments if they fulfil certain specified conditions.

'External elements' ('tier 2 capital') are defined as funds which are placed at the disposal of a credit institution but are not fully owned or controlled by it, or put at its disposal for a limited period only. No detailed list is given of these external elements, so that any developments can be included in it later, but the Directive does specifically mention subordinated loans and the liabilities of members of co-operative institutions in this context, and does lay down certain criteria which funds must meet to be included in the definition. By 1995, these external capital elements can only account for 50 per cent of an institution's own funds; half of them will have to be made up of internal elements.

The definition in this Directive is one of minimum prudence. Each member state is free to apply stricter criteria, applying lower ceilings for the amounts in question, or not including some of the elements listed in its own regulations. The Directive can be reviewed after it comes into force and amended to take account of new developments in the market. If, however, these amendments are substantial the full legislative procedure would have to be followed again.

The Solvency Ratio Directive

The purpose of this Directive is to establish a uniform minimum solvency ratio for all Community credit institutions, using capital defined in the Own Funds Directive as the numerator. This should both harmonize and strengthen EC solvency standards, as the requirements set out in it are generally more strict than those currently in use in many member states.

The solvency ratio of the Directive expresses own funds as a proportion of risk-adjusted assets and off-balance sheet transactions. This denominator is found by assigning different degrees of risk (risk-weightings) to each class of asset and off-balance sheet item, and then multiplying this weighting by the actual value and totalling these risk-adjusted values. It is generally accepted that this risk-adjusted approach to measuring institutions' solvency is the most flexible and appropriate one, because simpler ratios do not distinguish between different degrees of risk. For example, a loan to a home country government is far less risky than a loan to an individual, and therefore it is inappropriate to demand the same proportion of capital to cover these very different risks.

In order to assign risk weights, the Directive groups borrowers into broad categories, such as central banks, central governments and credit institutions. Borrowers in each category are further divided into 'domestic' (meaning EC) and 'foreign' (meaning non-EC) ones. The groups are then given risk-weightings of either 0 per cent, 10 per cent, 20 per cent, 50 per cent or 100 per cent according to a list included in the Directive. For most of the categories no distinction is made between domestic and foreign borrowers. However, in some cases (including central banks, central governments and long-term inter-bank business) domestic borrowers are given lower weightings than their foreign counterparts. This does not seem very appropriate, as it classes credit-worthy countries which happen not to be in the EC (such as Switzerland) together with less developed countries with massive financial problems. However, there is provision in the Directive for domestic weights to be extended to foreign borrowers if the risks are thought to be equivalent. When the borrower is a regional government or local authority the weights assigned to them by their home country supervisory authorities will be accepted by the lender's authorities.

The minimum level for the solvency ratio has been set at 8 per cent. However, this figure (together with the weightings of each asset group and other technical details) can be revised by the Commission, after consultations with the Banking Advisory Committee.

The Solvency Directive was adopted at the same time as the Second Banking Directive (December 1989), although institutions will not have to comply with the minimum ratio level until the beginning of 1993. But, those institutions which had a ratio level of below 8 per cent at the end of 1989 are not permitted to reduce the ratio further during this transition time, except in the specific instance of a capital issue. This is designed to strengthen capital standards in the period before the minimum ratio becomes binding on institutions.

Again, national supervisory authorities are allowed to impose higher capital standards on their domestic institutions than those set out in the Directive. However, it is only credit risk that is covered in the Directive, not market risk. Therefore, as has already been said, the authorities in each country still have responsibility for controlling market risk for all the credit institutions in their territory (host country control). A further directive has been proposed which will cover this type of risk, but it is very unlikely that it will be drafted for several years.

The provisions contained in both the Own Funds Directive and the Solvency Ratio Directive are consistent with those of the Basle agreement on capital adequacy made between the G10 leading industrial countries. There was close consultation between them, with the directives and the agreement being drawn up in parallel, and they are similar in all the most important aspects, including the capital definition, the risk-weightings and the minimum ratio. They also have to be complied with by the same date. Because of this, these harmonized standards will also apply beyond the EC to banks in the USA, Switzerland, Japan, Canada and Sweden.

The effect the requirements will have on Community institutions will depend on their present capital positions. Banks in several member states meet the minimum requirements already, and so will not be directly affected by them. However, many institutions will have to raise new capital and/or disclose their hidden reserves, and this may well limit their capacity for growth. IBCA Banking Analysis have estimated the current capital ratios of the G10 countries, and Table 4.2 shows the figures produced for those Community countries which are also members of G10. The figures in Table 4.2 show that institutions in Germany, Italy, the Netherlands, and the UK are already adequately capitalized. However, French and Belgian banks will have to take steps to improve their solvency ratios, as possibly will other Community banks.

OTHER COMMUNITY MEASURES

Two recommendations have also been issued to help harmonize and strengthen prudential standards among EC banks, as well as the Own Funds and Solvency Ratio directives. These recommendations are on large exposures and deposit-guarantee schemes. As was explained in Chapter 2, recommendations such as these are not legally binding on the credit institutions, but if banks do not comply with them they are liable to be replaced with directives.

Table 4.2 Current capital ratios

Country	Capital ratio
Belgium	7.5
France	7.5
Germany	9.0
Italy	8.6
The Netherlands	8.0
UK	8.0

Source: IBCA

An unacceptable concentration of risk can occur if a credit institution has an excessive degree of exposure with a single client or group of clients. This can threaten the protection of depositors and the bank's solvency. Therefore the Commission published a Recommendation on the Monitoring and Control of Large Exposures at the beginning of 1987. Institutions have to make an annual report to the supervisory authorities, detailing all large exposures (which are defined as more than 15 per cent of the institution's own funds), as well as their largest exposures, even if these are less than 15 per cent of their own funds.

A list is given in the Recommendation of items which constitute exposures. Both on-balance sheet loans and advances and off-balance sheet items, like guarantees and commitments, are included. Limits are also imposed on the size of exposures which may be incurred; specifically, 40 per cent of capital or 800 per cent of capital for the aggregate. Some types of exposures, however, are exempt from these limits, and member states can apply stricter requirements on their domestic institutions if they want to.

The Recommendation on Deposit-Guarantee Schemes was introduced at the same time. Deposit-guarantee schemes are meant to safeguard the interests of the depositors of an insolvent credit institution which is wound up. Under these schemes such depositors are guaranteed compensation or protection against any losses, and they are becoming increasingly important to maintain depositors' confidence in the financial markets. A directive proposed earlier had stated that guarantee schemes which institutions already took part in had to be extended to cover deposits in branches of those institutions in other member states where such schemes did not exist. This created an anomaly which could have led to a distortion of savings, and so this Recommendation was made to encourage those member states which did not have guarantee schemes to introduce them by 1990. Certain standards which the schemes had to meet were also set out.

The Commission has also tried to co-ordinate two other areas relating to banking by issuing directives. The first directive concerned the reorganization and winding-up of credit institutions, and attempted to co-ordinate the different laws, regulations and administrative procedures in the various countries. (This directive also extended deposit-guarantee schemes, as mentioned above.) Reorganization measures are those intended to safeguard or restore an institution's financial situation, and are listed in the Directive. It is the home country authorities which are responsible for implementing the measures necessary in these circumstances. When an institution operating in another country needs to be wound up both the home and host countries supervise the undertaking. When the institution is based outside the EC altogether the host country retains the right to reorganize or wind it up, if it is allowed to under its national law.

The second area is that of bank accounting requirements, both for the banks themselves and for their branches. With the cross-border provision of services becoming more widespread (and, obviously, with this trend going to increase greatly after 1992), the harmonization of the accounts of banks became very necessary.

Two directives on this matter have been adopted. The first is on the annual and consolidated accounts of banks and other financial institutions, and has to be implemented by credit institutions by 31 December 1990. It describes the layout, nomenclature, and terminology for the balance sheet and profit-and-loss account which banks should use, as well as of the consolidated accounts and the notes on the accounts. The Directive removes the preferential treatment on accounts that banks enjoyed in comparison to other businesses, and it greatly improves the comparability of banks' accounts in the member states.

The second directive is on the accounts of foreign branches, and lays down the accounting obligations of branches situated in member states with their head offices outside those states. Under the Directive, EC branches do not have to publish separate accounts as they used to but, instead, they have to produce consolidated accounts with the whole institution. Non-EC branches have to publish branch accounts only if their accounting documents are not the same as, or equivalent to, ones produced by EC banks, as defined in the Annual Accounts Directive. Therefore, third-country branches are basically treated in the same way as EC branches.

REMOVAL OF BARRIERS TO THE SECURITIES BUSINESS

Although the Second Banking Co-ordination Directive specifically includes securities and investment business in its list of activities covered by the single licence, the European Council has recognized that access to membership of some countries' stock exchanges, and other organized securities markets (for example, financial futures and options markets), does need to be liberalized. Nor does the Second Banking Directive cover non-bank investment firms, which are therefore put at a disadvantage to credit institutions in the range of cross-border services that they can provide. To remedy these deficiencies a proposed Council directive on investment services in the securities field was produced in December 1988.

Under this directive an investment firm is defined as 'any natural or legal person' whose business is to engage in one or more listed activities. These activities include market-making, brokerage, underwriting, portfolio management, and providing investment advice, in connection with a range of financial instruments: transferable securities, money market instruments (including certificates of deposit and Eurocommercial paper), financial futures and options, and exchange and interest rate instruments.

The proposed directive would allow investment companies to provide cross-border services on the same basis that the Second Banking Directive allows credit institutions to operate in different member states. Once an investment firm had been authorized to provide services in one EC country it could set up branches in other member states without needing additional authorization, without meeting separate capital requirements for each branch, and under the principle of home country control and regulation, although host country business conduct rules would still apply until their harmonization had been achieved. Reciprocity arrangements with investment firms from non-EC countries would be similar to those of the Second Banking Directive.

With regards to liberalizing access to stock exchange membership in host countries, the directive proposes three ways in which investment firms could obtain membership. The firm could become a direct member of the exchange by establishing a branch in the host state. Alternatively, the company could obtain membership indirectly either by creating a separately incorporated subsidiary in the country concerned, or by taking over an existing member of the exchange. In every case the host country's rules on the structure and organization of the exchange would have to be complied with. Barriers to stock exchange membership are not fully removed by the directive, however; those countries which do not allow credit institutions to become direct members of their exchanges still would not have to. In these cases credit institutions could obtain membership indirectly, through takeovers or by establishing subsidiaries.

Chapter 5
Banking strategies for 1992

A fully integrated financial market in the EC will present banks with a number of very important choices. They will be faced with both opportunities for new business and threats to their existing markets. The extent to which banks are affected by the removal of regulatory barriers by 1992 depends upon how they respond to the challenges posed. The effect that the single market will have on banks is twofold. First, the single market will have a direct effect on bank operations, by giving banks new opportunities to expand into other member states. Second, the market will affect the banks indirectly by changing the types of financial products and services that their customers will require.

Financial institutions throughout Europe are having to formulate their post-1992 operating strategies in order to minimize the threats to their business and to make the most of the new markets which will be open to them. Institutions have to decide, first, whether or not they should increase their present European activities (some may prefer instead to expand their share of the domestic market or non-EC markets such as the US and Japan). If institutions do decide upon European expansion they then have to choose what products to offer, which markets to target, and how to gain access to potential customers. As will be seen, these decisions have to be considered together, as the type of product will help determine both the market and the method of reaching customers.

This chapter will examine some of the strategies open to

banks and what some institutions are already doing in preparation, and Chapter 6 will look at the preparations of the major UK banks in particular.

RETAIL VS. WHOLESALE

Banking can be divided into retail (or personal) banking and wholesale (or corporate) banking. The choice of whether to offer retail or wholesale banking is a fundamental one, as the customers, financial products and services, and ways of providing those services are very different. Although most large banking groups (such as the Nat West group in the UK) conduct both retail and wholesale business, usually the different markets are served by separate companies within the group.

The retail/wholesale decision is crucial to banks' strategies for 1992. The profit margins available in the wholesale sector in Europe are much less than those which can be earned in the different retail markets in the Community. The wholesale sector is already fairly internationalized, both in terms of the products and services companies can make use of (for example, Eurobonds and exchange-rate hedging), and in terms of the institutions offering those services. Therefore competition for corporate business is intense.

In contrast, retail banking across Europe is fragmented and of varying degrees of sophistication (as was shown in the survey of the markets in Chapter 1). However, although the profits to be earned in some countries look very attractive, retail banking depends upon gaining large numbers of individual customers, which requires an extensive branch network. In the wholesale market a bank usually has comparatively few corporate clients, and, therefore, although the profits tend to be less, banks serving the wholesale market do not have the expense of running large branch networks. This illustrates what was said above, that the product, market and access decisions are inextricably linked.

WHAT PRODUCTS TO OFFER?

There are considerable differences between the financial markets in the EC: those of the UK, Germany and the Netherlands are highly developed and efficient, for example,

Table 5.1 Overview of payment systems and services in EEC member states, 1986

	UK	Fr	Ir	Be	Lu	Ne	Ge	Dn	Sp	It	Gr	Pt
Branches	W	H	W	H	H	H	H	W	W	L	L	L
Cheques	H	H	W	W	W	W	W	W	L	L	L	L
Cheque guarantee cards	H	L	W	H	H	H	H	W	L	L	L	L
Giro transfers	W	W	W	H	H	H	H	H	L	L	L	L
Pre-authorized payments	W	W	W	H	H	H	H	H	L	L	L	L
Credit cards	H	W	W	W	L	L	L	L	W	L	L	L
ATMs	H	H	W	W	L	V	L	L	W	L	V	V
EFTPOS	V	L	N	L	E	E	E	L	L	E	N	N

H: High   W: Widespread   L: Limited   V: Very limited   E: Experimental   N: Non-existent.
Source: Vittas (1987) *New Products and Electronic Funds Transfer and the Stakes in Europe*

while those of Spain, Greece and Portugal are not. This means that the extent to which particular products are available differs markedly between the states. Table 5.1 illustrates this by showing the differences in usage of various methods of payment in the EC. The use of cheques and credit cards, for instance, is limited in the Mediterranean countries, but very widespread in Belgium, France, Ireland and the UK. It is this current diversity in national financial markets which will give institutions opportunities to expand into other countries and markets.

However, banks are highly unlikely to offer the entire range of banking services and products in the markets they choose to target, or to offer exactly the same products in all the member states, and they would be very foolish to attempt to do so. The products offered in each market will have to be carefully selected, in order to meet the needs of that market. If the particular service or product has not been available before in that country, or if the domestic market is uncompetitive and therefore expensive, or if the take-up rate of the product is still low there, then the market will present opportunities for new players. However, a Community-wide market will probably not develop for many products, because of differences in habit and culture, and the difficulties of distribution. Successful expansion for banks is likely to come either through focusing on a particular need in a particular area, or through product

Table 5.2 Cost of consumer credit

Country	Cost
Belgium	2.3
Denmark	9.2
France	8.0
Luxembourg	2.8
Netherlands	5.1
Spain	5.4
UK	8.6

differentiation. Compagnie Bancaire of Paris has already begun to offer French-style fixed-rate mortgages in the UK, and British-style variable-rate ones in France!

In order to give an idea of some of the factors that have to be considered when a bank is deciding upon its product strategy (such as market needs, price differentials, the costs of provision, etc.), a few products are looked at in general terms below.

Consumer credit

Consumer credit provision is limited in some member states, and a bank does not actually require a large branch network to provide it (although a substantial market share might be difficult to gain without one). Newcomers to a particular market could find themselves at a disadvantage compared with the domestic retail banks when assessing credit risks, but there do seem to be possibilities for expansion in this area for UK banks. However, comparative product prices in the markets also have to be looked at. Table 5.2 details the average costs of consumer credit in eight EC countries, as shown in the Cecchini Report (see pp. 99-106).

These costs are measured as the average per annum rate of interest charged above money market rates, and so are not the actual costs incurred by consumers. However, as the single market is expected to reduce the differences between interest rates in member states (see p. 107), the effect of national interest rates will be lessened.

Although there are many methodological problems associated with the figures produced in the Cecchini report (which are discussed on p. 103), Table 5.2 shows how the UK and Denmark are at present the most expensive countries for

Table 5.3 Mortgage costs in the EC

Country	Cost
Belgium	1.92
Denmark	2.30
France	2.61
Italy	1.40
Netherlands	1.37
Spain	3.20
UK	1.16

consumer credit, and Luxembourg and Belgium the cheapest. Therefore, it is unlikely that UK banks could sell credit successfully abroad, and it is probable that it is the reverse that will happen – Continental banks will compete for a share of the UK consumer credit market instead.

Mortgages

UK banks and building societies are in a much stronger position, though, when it comes to mortgages (see Table 5.3). The Cecchini Report calculated that the UK was the cheapest country in the Community for mortgage finance (again when costs were calculated as the excess of average percentage interest rates charged over money market rates). The UK mortgage market has the advantages of fewer restrictions than most other EC markets, and more readily available finance.

However, banks wanting to expand into foreign mortgage markets will come up against non-regulatory barriers, which will be very hard to break down. At present national mortgage techniques, mortgage terms, and the institutions they are obtained from vary widely across the EC. One example is the widespread Continental distrust of variable mortgage rates. These are banned outright in Belgium, and are restricted in other countries. Even if these restrictions are lifted people will probably stick with those institutions and practices with which they are familiar, especially where such a major, long-term commitment as a mortgage is concerned. Success in the mortgage market is far more dependent upon an established customer base, and good name awareness, reputation, and distribution network than success in other markets is. (This was shown to work both ways when the banks entered the housing market in Britain: they had no experience of providing mortgages, but rapidly gained a large share of the market, simply because everyone had heard of them and they had branches everywhere.)

Restrictions on mortgage lending may also still remain in certain countries after the single market comes into operation. The Second Banking Co-ordination Directive does specifically cover mortgage lending by credit institutions, and as it lays down that host country control is to remain in force for the conduct of business rules and consumer protection measures, member states may still refuse to allow particular mortgage techniques on these grounds.

All these factors mean that mortgage markets will probably remain fairly national ones. Some institutions may try to exploit niche markets in other countries (for example, expatriate markets, or markets for holiday homes in Spain and Portugal, especially among the British). However, in general, the housing market in Europe does not seem to be as attractive for new foreign players as it did at first.

Corporate banking

Certain aspects of corporate finance offer opportunities in Europe for banks, despite the fact that the wholesale market is largely an international one already. UK banks will be in a good position to offer Continental customers specialized services, such as portfolio management and advice, because of their unique access and participation in the London money markets. However, investment services may be slower to open up than other banking business; while banks are covered for this type of business by the Second Banking Directive, non-banks are not, and so cannot take advantage of the single banking licence. An investment services directive will probably be passed by the Commission at some stage in order to redress this inequality.

WHICH AREAS TO TARGET?

Just as banks are unlikely to try to provide the entire range of banking services and products in the single market most are very unlikely to establish pan-European presences, at least in the near future. Although many banks have some personnel in all the EC countries, often this consists merely of a representative office. To establish a viable market share in each member state would be almost impossible for any bank. Even if two of the largest banks in Europe at present, National Westminster and Deutsche Bank (ranked first and fifth by capital respectively at the end of 1988) merged, they would still have only 6 per cent of the total European market (according to Philip Young of Nat West's Business Development Division).

The very different cultural regions which make up Europe would also make it difficult for banks to establish operations successfully throughout the EC. For instance, the Mediterranean countries of Spain, Portugal and Italy have a very different culture and way of life from that of Germany, the Netherlands and Flemish Belgium, which can be grouped together to form another region. It will undoubtedly be easier for financial institutions to expand their business into countries which have a similar cultural identity to their home country than into countries with marked cultural differences. However, some member states seem to have rather more in common with countries which are outside the Community, such as Scandinavian Denmark, than they do with their EC partners.

Again, it has to be remembered that strategy decisions are interrelated. Certain countries will present banks with opportunities for selling certain products because of the state of their particular financial markets. The banks will have to decide in which market they can operate most profitably. The Cecchini survey identified various products which could be promoted most profitably in certain countries. For example, in Italy there are opportunities for banks to sell credit cards, insurance, securities and consumer credit; in Germany mortgages, consumer credit and credit cards; and in Spain letters of credit, mortgages and foreign exchange business.

HOW TO GAIN ACCESS TO CUSTOMERS?

The question of gaining access to potential customers abroad is crucial to banks' European expansion strategies. Many products and services, especially those provided in retail banking, require the bank to have a market presence to sell them, although some can be provided successfully by cross-border trading. These latter products are much less expensive for the bank to market than those which have to be sold directly in the particular area, and there are also several different ways (of varying degrees of complexity and costliness) of setting up a market presence. Therefore the way in which a bank reaches its customers has a great influence on the eventual profitability of the product and market.

There are three main ways of establishing a market presence abroad:

1 By building new branches in the particular countries (the 'green fields' or 'organic growth' approach);
2 Through merging with or taking over financial institutions already established in the market; or
3 By developing business links with foreign banks and financial institutions.

The 'green fields' approach

This is the most expensive and time-consuming of the three methods. Very large amounts of capital have to be invested to build up a viable branch network across the markets, and even after the network is built it still takes a long time for the bank to gain business and a share of the market from the existing domestic institutions. There may also be problems with finding staff with the required local knowledge and expertise.

Mergers and acquisitions

Merging with or acquiring a foreign bank is a much more attractive option than setting up a branch network from scratch. It is far quicker; a customer base already exists; the general public are aware of the local bank's name, so the acquiring institution does not have to spend time building up its reputation and acceptance; and the branch managers will already have a good knowledge of the local market. There are disadvantages of course – different management cultures and systems could make it difficult to integrate the two institutions, and it could also be fairly expensive (though less so than the 'green fields' method). Heavy premiums on book values normally have to be paid when European banks are bought.

Cross-border mergers and acquisitions in the run-up to 1992 may still be hampered by national regulatory barriers, as national takeover codes tend to be most strict when dealing with the sensitive area of domestic financial services. The majority of member states impose regulatory requirements for acquisitions of domestic banks or participations in them by foreign institutions. In the UK the Bank of England has to approve all such acquisitions, and this approval is only given if both parties agree to the takeover; and if the Bank is satisfied as to the foreign bank's capital position, management reputation and future intentions. However, some countries impose much tougher restrictions. For example, in Spain the purchase by a foreign bank of more than 50 per cent of a domestic institution will be approved only in very exceptional circumstances, usually when the target is a distressed bank.

A Community takeover code has been proposed by the Commission, but it does not specifically cover the takeover of banks and other financial institutions. It is possible that national bank takeover codes will still operate after the single market has come into force. If the Commission does propose that national barriers against bank takeovers by other EC institutions be removed there will probably be considerable opposition from the individual supervisory authorities. The Bank of England, for one, has stated that it regards it as very important that a substantial part of the UK financial services industry should remain under British control.

A strategy of acquiring or merging with foreign banks might also be difficult because of the lack of suitable targets. Many of the largest banks in Europe are owned by national governments or are of mutual or co-operative status, and so cannot be acquired by hostile takeover bids. Table 5.4 shows the status of the top 162 Community banks in 1988. Only 69 are privately owned and so can be subject to a hostile bid, and many of these are either too large and nationally important to be taken over by a foreign institution, or are already subsidiaries of other banks and so are not likely to be bought by any other group.

Table 5.4 Status of top 162 EC banks in 1988

Status	Number
Private	69
Public (central/local government)	67
Co-operatives	14
Mutuals	12

Source: The Banker, July 1988

Business links

The strategy of co-operating with banks in other countries for mutual advantage has probably the biggest potential of all of the ones discussed. The participants gain access to an established customer base and branch network, and can take advantage of the other bank's reputation, strengths, and local expertise, while avoiding the cost and regulatory requirements involved in a full acquisition or merger (although there might be a token exchange of minority equity stakes to seal the agreement and show good faith).

The most beneficial link-ups would be between institutions with different specialisms, so that each could offer the other's products and services through their branches without creating more competition for itself. Another advantage of this method of establishing a foreign market presence is that the bank's international service to its existing customers is improved, as they can use the branches and services of the other bank when travelling or trading abroad.

CURRENT BANK STRATEGIES

To prepare for the opening up of the European banking market, banks are tending to opt for some sort of link-up with other institutions, either foreign or domestic, in order to expand their business into new areas and countries or to strengthen themselves and their markets against hostile takeovers. Not surprisingly, the one strategy which does not seem to be popular at the moment is that of organic growth abroad. The Executive Director of Overseas Operations from Barclays Bank summed up the problem with it in a recent speech:

We have, in round figures, 3,000 branches in the UK but only just over 200 branches throughout the rest of the EC. To replicate our UK network across Europe would require, say 12,000 additional branches, with a total investment of something like £12 billion. No bank can afford, or justify, such expense.

Cross-border links

In the last two or three years there has been a rash of various kinds of link-ups (takeovers, mergers, business links, etc.) between banks of different countries. The majority of these link-ups have been takeovers of comparatively small banks by very much larger banks. Because of the difficulties associated with the takeover of large, national banks (mentioned on p. 84), any links between these tend to be effected through either mergers or co-operative agreements.

A handful of the biggest European banks (such as Deutsche Bank, Crédit Lyonnaise, and Paribas) are aiming to set up pan-European banking groups, offering wide ranges of both retail and corporate banking services. Deutsche Bank provides an interesting example. It is following a three-pronged expansion plan to prepare for 1992: retail banking operations in Europe (especially for high net-worth customers); investment banking services worldwide; and the provision of a range of related services, such as insurance (mainly in Germany at present). To achieve this, within the last two years Deutsche Bank has bought or established operations in Spain, Italy, Switzerland, the UK, Luxembourg, Argentina, Singapore and Indonesia. The acquisitions (Deutsche has avoided getting involved in cross-border mergers or share exchanges) have all been very carefully planned. The bank does not buy indiscriminately, but makes sure that the target fits in with the overall business of Deutsche and its expansion strategy. For example, it expanded its retail banking in Italy by taking over Banca d'America e d'Italia in December 1986, a subsidiary of Bank of America and the eighth largest bank in Italy. To strengthen its corporate and investment banking, Deutsche bought out its existing partners in a Portuguese merchant bank and, in its biggest deal to date, it made a £950 million takeover of the UK bank Morgan Grenfell at the end of 1989. Under this deal, Deutsche will benefit from Morgan's fund management and corporate finance expertise, with Morgan's present corporate banking management team becoming responsible for all Deutsche's business in this field.

Other cross-border takeovers have followed the same pattern of acquiring either a retail distribution network in another member state, or an institution with a complementary business (such as insurance or fund management) in order to expand the predator's range of activities. Examples of such takeovers are that of Nederlandse Credietbank (the Dutch subsidiary of Chase Manhattan) by Crédit Lyonnaise at the end of 1987; Banque Crédit Commercial of Belgium by Spain's Banco Bilbao Vizcaya; and in the UK the takeovers of the leasing company Humberclyde Investment by Compagnie Bancaire, fund managers Foreign and Colonial by Bayerische Hypotheken- & Wechsel-Bank, Touche Remnant by Société Generale, and Cornhill Insurance by the German insurance giants Allianz. Dresdner Bank also considered a £1 billion takeover of Britain's twelfth largest bank, Yorkshire.

Several cross-border mergers and business links have taken place as well. These mostly occur between institutions of a similar size, either as a defence against hostile takeovers, or to pool resources in order to improve offensive positions. Mergers and business agreements are also ways in which national banks can avoid the regulations on takeovers and work together. For example, a merger was proposed between Belgium's largest bank (Generale Bank) and the third largest Dutch bank, Amsterdam-Rotterdam Bank (AMRO). In February 1988 each bank took a 25 per cent equity stake in the other, as a first step to becoming 'a fully integrated banking unit' within three years. The merged bank would have become the eighth largest in Europe. However, the deal eventually fell through, although the banks still have a 5 per cent equity stake in each other, and are still co-operating informally.

Most of the arrangements between Europe's large banks consist of share swaps and reciprocal agreements, rather than full mergers, at least at this stage. Commerzbank and Crédit Lyonnaise (the third biggest banks in Germany and France) have made a 10 per cent equity swap, and propose to offer each other's products through their banks, so improving their customer service and European distribution. Another German and French pairing, Dresdner Bank and the state-owned Banque Nationale de Paris, have also made co-operative arrangements, swapping board members. BNP is working with Spain's largest banking group (Banco Bilbao Vizcaya) as well. They have swapped 85 branches each, so that they can both build up their distribution networks in the other's country.

Cross-border mergers between similar institutions have also been happening. For example, the rural banks in Spain (*cajas rurales*) have formed a link with the German DG Bank, which is the umbrella organization for the German co-operative banks. A joint venture has been created (Banco Co-operativo Espanol) between the two, with the *cajas* having a majority control over the new bank.

Internal mergers

As well as the cross-border takeovers and mergers, there has been a number of mergers between institutions of the same country (especially in Spain, Germany and the Netherlands) in order to create more powerful national groupings which are less vulnerable to foreign takeover. The Spanish government has been encouraging its financial institutions to team-up to try to improve efficiency and reduce costs, and so make the banking system better able to withstand the expected increased competition of the single market. Spain's biggest bank (ranked seventeenth in Europe by capital) was created by the merger of the two Basque banks, Banco de Bilbao and Banco de Vizcaya (the country's third and sixth largest banks respectively). In the Netherlands, NMB bank has just merged with the recently fully privatized Postbank, and the largest Dutch savings bank (Verenigde Spaarbank) has proposed a merger with the large insurance institution Amev.

The German *Landesbanks* (savings banks) have concluded several mergers between themselves; for example, that between Landesbank Stuttgart and Bayerische Kommunale Landesbank (Bakola). There were also merger talks between two large regional savings banks (Westdeutsche Landesbank and Hessiche Landesbank), but these came to nothing; the resulting institution would have been larger than Dresdner Bank.

SERVING EXISTING CUSTOMERS

As well as planning how to take advantage of the new opportunities opening up to them in Europe, banks will also have to consider how the single market will affect their existing customers, and what sort of new and better services they will be demanding from their banks. It is expected that 1992 will have the greatest effect on smaller and medium-sized companies. The removal of barriers will promote their expansion abroad, and will also probably mean a great deal of restructuring among industries. It will be these customers who will be turning increasingly to their banks for help and advice, and so the banks will have to improve their international services in order to retain this business.

Changing demands

Businesses will expect to have full access to their bank in all the Community countries in which they operate – i.e. to a branch conducting banking business, rather than to a representative office. Therefore, increasingly banks will have to set up a market presence throughout the EC to serve corporate customers. Banks which decide to concentrate on this, rather than on gaining a new customer base abroad, will probably find that the most effective way is through co-operative links with other national banks.

Co-operative agreements will also give banks (and their clients) access to information and knowledge on the local markets and customs. As businesses are expected to need far more expert financial advice on their European operations, and on European mergers and acquisitions procedures as companies expand and restructure, this local knowledge will be vital for corporate customers.

There will be an increase in demand for import/export banking services as well, such as payments transmission, foreign exchange, short- and medium-term export finance, the negotiation and collection of bills of exchange, and documentary letters of credit. Banks will have to improve their provision of these services, or risk losing business to other institutions.

Payment systems

One particular area where banks are going to have to make great improvements is that of payment and money transmission services. Trade within the Community is expected to grow substantially because of the single market programme, and so there will be much greater demand for cross-border payments than there is at present. Ideally, people should be able to pay for goods, and receive payment for transactions, on the same day throughout the Community, using their normal bank accounts. However, at present money transmission within the EC is appallingly inefficient. A study by BEUC (the EC consumers' association) found that the average time it took to transfer £70 from one member state to another was five days – the range being between one day and five months, with some of the payments never arriving at all! The average banking commission charged on these transactions was 9 per cent, and there was a lot of uncertainty about whether this was to be paid by the money's sender or receiver. It is feared that, unless these money transmissions are substantially improved, smaller and medium-sized businesses will be discouraged from expanding their cross-border activities.

Electronic payments systems should also be expanded and improved, because of the increase in cross-border trade by smaller companies. These payments systems are currently available to large corporate customers for a range of instruments and transactions. Banks would greatly improve their level of service to smaller companies if they made these facilities open to them as well. However, creating a fully electronic cross-border payments system would be very expensive and fairly complicated: the diverse payments systems already operating would have to be linked together, and agreements would have to be made between the different national and international clearing houses.

There is scope for banks to improve their services to their individual customers, as well as to their corporate clients. The removal of internal barriers will encourage the free movement of individuals throughout the Community, and an improved plastic card service would help this process. At present, foreign currency notes can be obtained from a large number of ATMs across the EC, and the Commission wants to develop this. In 1987 it published its strategy on plastic cards and payments systems, with the aim, finally, of allowing holders of cards issued in one member state access to services supplied in another. A number of technical problems will have to be solved first, either by making the different systems compatible or by standardizing the cards (which now are either smart cards or magnetic strip ones).

One important step was made in October 1987, when the European Council for Payment Systems (a non-Community body) reached an agreement for creating a Europe-wide plastic card standard. This consists of making the Visa and Mastercard systems compatible, and setting up a single electronic network, connecting bank-owned ATM and EFTPOS terminals throughout the EC but still preserving bank competition. An integrated network is technically perfectly possible: in the UK the ATMs of Midland and Nat West, and those of Barclays, Lloyds, the Bank of Scotland and the Royal Bank of Scotland have been linked for a number of years. The ECPS agreement is concerned with access to a technological infrastructure of electronic highways between ATMs, cash dispensers and point-of-sales terminals. The agreement may be blocked, however, by the Commission, because it excludes access by non-bank financial services companies which offer payment cards (such as Diners Club and American Express), and these organizations have already made numerous complaints to the Commission.

Compatible systems would allow banks to improve greatly their international services to individual customers, without needing to invest enormous amounts of capital in the work. Co-operative links between different banks often involve sharing their respective technology and electronic networks.

Chapter 6
Preparations and attitudes of the major UK banks

THE PREPARATIONS OF BRITISH BANKS

In common with banks all over Europe, banks in the UK are busy preparing for the opening up of the financial services market at the end of 1992. For competitive reasons, many of the public statements made by banks about their future European strategies are so general as to be bordering on banality. Examples of such statements include 'we aim to significantly expand our presence in Europe', and 'we are actively assessing the opportunities available'. All the major British banks (in both the retail and wholesale sectors) were contacted about their plans for 1992, and although few of the banks revealed any details, most of them were extremely helpful, and it has been possible to build up some idea of how UK banks are approaching the advent of the single market.

Expansion into Europe

All the major British banks have decided to increase their European operations to some degree, even though some of them already conduct significant amounts of business in Europe, especially in the corporate sector. As with the Continental banks mentioned in the last chapter, the UK institutions are tending to favour strategic alliances and the takeover of smaller banks and branch networks as methods of building up a market presence, rather than the green fields approach. However, unlike some other major European banks (such as Deutsche Bank and Paribas), the big British banks, like National Westminster (the largest bank in Europe by capital), are not at present trying to establish themselves as pan-European universal financial institutions, offering all banking services to all Europeans. They are tending to focus instead on those specific products and regions which their research has indicated as offering the most potential.

The Nat West, for example, has decided to concentrate on the markets of Spain, France, Germany, the Netherlands and northern Italy. Its plans were summed up at the end of 1989 by its Head of Strategy for European Business, David Brice: 'We're looking to be a scale player in European retail business. To be one we need customer base, distribution network, product range [sic]. That means to me that most of our plans will involve acquisition.' (*The Banker*, November 1989). To this end, Nat West recently bought over an 80 per cent stake in each of two Spanish banks, Banco Nat West March and Banco d'Asturias. In 1988 it acquired five branches of Banque de l'Union Européenne in France (together with the French stockbroking company Selier), and a minority stake in the Italian Banca Credit West e dei Comuni Vesuviani. Currently, the bank is negotiating with Rabobank of the Netherlands to buy 40 per cent of the latter's shares in the eighth largest Dutch bank, F. von Lanschot Bankiers.

These acquisitions have given Nat West access to established customer bases. Two sectors the bank is concentrating on in particular are medium-sized corporate clients and high net-worth retail customers. Both are sections of the market which can be served through a fairly limited branch network (certainly through a less extensive network than that needed to serve the *hoi polloi* of the mass retail market), and in which a bank offering a high quality, customized service can gain a significant market share.

Barclays is another UK bank which favours selective acquisitions. Its Executive Director of Overseas Operations has said of the bank's plans that 'the first thing we concluded early on was that we did not need monumental acquisitions or major strategic alliances'. The advantages arising from these were not thought to be great enough to justify the time and cost of such a policy, and it was felt that some of the

Continental banks (especially French and German ones) would have to curtail their current buying sprees in order to meet the new solvency ratios directed by the Commission.

Barclays has made some acquisitions, however, for example in Spain, and it is linking up with locally based institutions to market its Barclaycard credit cards directly in different European countries, rather than through cross-border selling. All the administration, debt collection, and application processing connected with the cards will be carried out separately in each market. By doing this Barclays is hoping to gain a share of local retail markets by cross-selling its other products, tailored for each different market, via its cards and local contacts.

The Royal Bank of Scotland provides an example of a UK bank pursuing major business alliances with other European banks based on equal partnerships. In 1987 it teamed up with the fourth largest bank in Spain, Banco Santander. The two banks are of a similar size. In 1988 Santander had total assets of nearly $30 billion and Royal of $36 billion, and their profits that year were $560 million and $520 million respectively. More importantly, as the Chairman of Santander noted at the time, the banks 'share a common culture which emphasizes profitability and efficiency'. A 2.5 per cent equity swap was made, but both banks have always stated that a merger between them has never been contemplated; although Santander increased its stake in the Royal Bank to 10 per cent in 1989 (with Royal's permission – neither bank can buy or sell shares in the other without its approval), the RBS still has voting control over these shares.

The key features of the alliance are:

1 *Branch access.* The RBS has 850 branches throughout the UK, but in Europe it has only one Swiss subsidiary and an office in Greece. However, Banco Santander has the largest branch network in Europe of all the Spanish banks, with over 1,450 outlets in Spain, 33 in Germany and 21 in Belgium. With this agreement each bank can offer its services through the other's branches. The RBS, therefore, can greatly improve the service it can give to British companies, tourists and expatriates in Spain (and

to a lesser extent in Belgium and Germany), and Santander can do likewise in the UK.
2 *Shared ownership of German and Belgian banks.* The alliance provides for RBS to acquire a 50 per cent stake in both the German and Belgian subsidiaries of Santander. Santander has retained responsibility for the day-to-day control and management of them, but the two banks are working together to develop the businesses.
3 *Investment banking.* The investment banking sections of the two banks are co-operating to provide European M&A, management buy-out, and stockbroking services.
4 *Technology.* RBS and Santander are sharing their existing technology and equipment; for example Santander's ATMs are being adapted to take Royal's Cashline cards, and are developing new projects together.
5 *Joint ventures.* Joint acquisitions are planned in Europe (like the 49.8 per cent stake the two banks hold between them in the Portuguese Banco de Comercio e Industria), as well as the establishment of an offshore banking service in Gibraltar, to serve high net-worth British and Spanish expatriates there.

The Royal Bank is now trying to form additional alliances with other banks, to give it access to the French, Dutch and Italian markets, now that it has these toe-holds in Europe.

The business-link approach has also been used by the merchant bank Hambros. It has joined up with several European institutions, including Bayerische Vereinsbank, Banco Bilbao Vizcaya, the Institute Bancario San Paolo in Italy, and a M & A specialist in Denmark. The main purpose behind these links for Hambros is to allow its Euro M & A department to make use of local specialists and contacts, so that it can provide a very effective and competitive service to its clients. The growth in cross-border mergers and acquisitions which 1992 is expected to bring has prompted virtually all the UK's merchant banks to expand and develop their Euro M & A departments. Hill Samuel is another institution which has built up a network of business associates in other member states. Others, like Morgan Grenfell, S. G. Warburg, and Rothschilds, have opened up new offices in various countries.

Barclays de Zoete Wedd (the merchant banking subsidiary of Barclays plc) has bought controlling holdings in a number of European brokerage houses. It acquired 70 per cent of the French stockbrokers Puget at the end of 1987, and it has taken over two other broking firms, one in Spain and one in the Netherlands, both fellow subsidiaries of Barclays.

Midland Bank has also been expanding its activities in Europe, buying a controlling equity share in an Italian investment bank, Euromobiliare. Midland's strategy for retail business is technology-based; for example, providing 24-hour telephone banking through its subsidiary 'first direct'. For corporate clients the bank aims to establish a reputation for providing expert financial advice on expansion and defensive strategies in the single market, as well as to expand its provision of foreign exchange and treasury services, business travel facilities, and electronic and card payments.

Other preparations

Establishing wider European presences is not the only way UK banks are preparing for 1992. One other way is through changes in their internal organization. Barclays, for example, has replaced the old, geographically based management structure of its European activities (where each country's operations were managed in relative isolation to those of other countries) with a matrix management structure. Market segmentation has been adopted, with the management of retail business being separated from that of corporate business. Two new directors have also been appointed. The European Director, Retail Services has responsibility for researching and developing personal banking in the member states, and the job of the European Director, Corporate Services is to co-ordinate the marketing and operation of Barclays' investment and treasury services on the Continent. Like the Nat West, Barclays is concentrating on the upper-end of the personal market, and on medium-sized corporate customers. The bank is aiming to create specialist business centres for these corporate clients wherever it is recognized that areas have a concentration of such medium-sized businesses.

Other banks have also carried out internal reorganization to prepare for the single market. Some have appointed a manager within their international division to be specifically responsible for matters relating to 1992. Nat West has taken this a stage further. It has set up an entire '1992 Policy Unit'.

Staff recruitment is beginning to be geared towards the single market as well. Barclays de Zeote Wedd is operating graduate recruitment programmes in several member states, and aims to employ people who can speak the main EC languages. Hambros has also recruited a multilingual team, with European expertise, for its M & A department.

Another way in which banks are preparing for 1992 is by developing and diversifying their UK operations; for example, by expanding into related financial areas, such as insurance. The Royal Bank of Scotland and the mutual life company Scottish Equitable set up a joint life assurance venture in 1989, and Lloyds Bank has a majority stake in the Abbey Life company. Lloyds has diversified into the estate agency business, too, as have other institutions, such as Abbey National and the Prudential insurance company. Prudential are also trying to take over one of the medium-sized building societies, in order to establish a retail network for pensions, insurance, investment planning and deposit-taking. A final example of this domestic diversification is provided by the leading stockbroking company, Cazanove and Co. It has gradually been developing merchant banking facilities (such as a mergers department) in order to turn itself into an integrated investment bank, rather than remain a pure broking operation.

Chapter 7

Economic aspects of a single market in financial services

The economic implications of the overall internal market programme were examined in Chapter 2. In this chapter the economic consequences of an internal financial market will be discussed specifically.

THE CECCHINI REPORT

In 1986 a report for the European Commission was produced under the supervision of Paolo Cecchini, entitled *The Cost of Non-Europe – Basic Findings*. It consisted of 16 volumes and examined the effects that the remaining barriers in the Community had on the European economy, as well as calculating the potential gains that would come about by their removal. Volume 9, produced by Price Waterhouse, dealt with the financial sector. It estimated the expected gains in consumer surplus that could result from a free Community market in credit and insurance, by studying the existing price differentials and using these figures to estimate likely price changes in the future.

Existing and future price levels

The price levels for a range of standardized financial products and services in eight member states – France, Germany, Italy, Spain, the UK and the Benelux countries – were examined. The products were chosen to be representative of the financial

Table 7.1 Percentage difference in prices from the average of the four lowest national prices

	Be	Fr	Ge	It	Lu	Ne	Sp	UK
Banking:								
Consumer credit	−41	n.a.	136	121	−26	31	39	121
Credit cards	79	−30	60	89	−12	43	26	16
Mortgages	31	78	57	−4	n.a.	−6	118	−20
Travellers cheques	35	39	−7	22	−7	33	30	−7
Letters of credit	22	−7	−10	9	27	17	59	8
Foreign exchange	6	56	31	23	33	−46	196	16
Commercial loans	−5	−7	6	9	6	43	19	46
Implied potential fall	16	25	33	18	16	10	34	18
Assumed potential fall	8	13	13	9	8	5	20	9
Total financial market:								
Implied potential fall	23	24	25	29	17	9	34	13
Assumed potential fall	11	12	10	14	8	4	21	7

Source: *The Cost of Non-Europe in Financial Services* (1986). Vol. 9 of (The Cecchini Report) *The Cost of Non-Europe – Basic Findings*, EC Commission: Brussels.

sector as a whole, and are listed and described in Appendix II. The report found that the price levels of the products differed widely between the member states, especially for mortgages, consumer credit, motor insurance and securities. Some countries were consistently relatively expensive across the whole range of products, while other countries were comparatively expensive for some services, but cheap for others. Britain, for example, was the most expensive country (bar Germany) for consumer credit, while at the same time being the cheapest of the states for mortgage finance. The detailed results for both mortgage finance and consumer credit were given in Chapter 5.

The report then estimated future price levels from the existing levels. To do this, factors such as value added/output ratios in the banking and insurance sectors, and the net margins for the main groups of credit and insurance institutions in each country were taken into consideration, together with a case study on the impact of deregulation in the UK securities market. However, obviously, the estimates produced were speculative, and a number of possible calculation methods could have been used. Under the one which was, the average of the four lowest prices observed was taken to be the price that would prevail under conditions of complete liberalization and identical market conditions. The difference between this average price and the actual prices observed for each country was calculated. These differences were then converted into potential price falls for each sector, and for the industry as a whole, using a weighting system. Each service was weighted according to its estimated relative economic importance.

However, different national conditions contribute to price differences, as do regulatory barriers, and so the differences will not be completely eliminated when the single market is in place. Therefore, the potential price falls which had been calculated would overestimate the economic gains which could be attained. To allow for this overestimation, these 'implied potential price reductions' were scaled down by between 40 and 60 per cent (depending upon national conditions), in order to obtain the 'assumed potential price reductions'.

Table 7.1 shows the detailed results calculated for the banking sector, and the summarized results for the financial market as a whole.

It should be noted that the figures in Table 7.1 are, in many cases, based on costs in excess of money market rates, rather than on actual costs to the consumer, and so do not represent absolute reductions in consumer price. The reductions in real consumer prices would be considerably less than these assumed price reductions.

Gains in consumer surplus

The increase in consumer surplus that would result from each country was then estimated, using the above assumptions on future price changes, together with assumptions on the elasticity of demand for financial services and value added. To allow for a wide margin of error, ranges of price falls of ±5 per cent of the estimates were used, and so upper and lower figures for the gains in consumer surplus were calculated. Table 7.2 shows the gains resulting from the integration of the credit and insurance sectors as a whole.

The gains in consumer surplus were calculated separately also for the banking and insurance sectors but, because of differences in definitions, the results for the individual sectors do not equate with the aggregated results. The estimated gains

Table 7.2 Gains in consumer surplus

	ECUs billion Range	Point estimate*
Belgium	0.4–1.1	0.7
France	2.1–5.3	3.7
Germany	2.3–7.1	4.6
Italy	2.5–5.5	4.0
Luxembourg	0.0–0.1	0.1
The Netherlands	0.1–0.8	0.3
Spain	2.4–4.0	3.2
UK	1.4–8.8	5.1
Total		21.7

Note: * This estimate is that calculated from the mid-point of the price range used, and is not necessarily the mid-point of the estimated range of gains in consumer surplus.

Table 7.3 Gains in consumer surplus, banking sector

	ECUs billion Range	Mid-point*
Belgium	0.2–0.6	0.4
France	1.9–4.9	3.4
Germany	2.4–6.2	4.3
Italy	1.2–3.8	2.5
The Netherlands	0.1–0.7	0.4
Spain	1.5–2.5	2.0
UK	0.9–3.2	2.0
Total		15.0

Source: The Cost of Non-Europe in Financial Services, (1986). Vol. 9 of (The Cecchini Report) *The Cost of Non-Europe – Basic Findings*, EC Commission: Brussels
Note: * As no point estimate was given for these figures, the mid-point of the range of estimated gains has been used as an approximation (this explains the apparent contradiction between the point estimates for the Netherlands). No figures were given for Luxembourg.

from the integration of the banking markets are given in Table 7.3.

The overall increase, therefore, in consumer surplus for the European economy due to the single financial market was estimated to be between 11 billion and 33 billion ECU (between £7.7 billion and £23.1 billion). The integration of the banking sector was estimated to account for between 8 billion and 22 billion ECU of this. The largest overall benefits were expected to occur in the UK, even though the expected price falls were among the lowest of the eight countries. This was because the size of the financial sector in the UK means that relatively small percentage price reductions become greatly magnified, resulting in a large gain overall. The 5.1 billion ECU total gain represents approximately 0.8 per cent of the UK's gross domestic product.

It is emphasized in the report that the figures indicate possible benefits to consumers and not impact on economic activity, as the effects of redistribution between different producers and different countries are not taken into account. Although companies are expected to become more efficient because of market integration, a proportion of the price reductions will cause a decrease in producer surplus. Therefore, in order to use the figures in this report to estimate gains in overall economic welfare it would be necessary to subtract estimates for this decline in producer surplus from the gains in consumer surplus. The report does present a methodology for doing this, which produces a total gain in net economic welfare of 22 billion ECU – a substantial micro-economic gain.

Methodological problems

There are a large number of methodological problems associated with the Cecchini study, many of which are mentioned in the report itself. It is frequently stressed in the study that the results should be used with caution. Some of these problems have been pointed out already, such as the fact that the prices quoted do not represent actual consumer cost, and the way in which differences in the definitions used create discrepancies between the estimates for gains in consumer surplus for the entire credit and insurance sector and the sum of the estimates for the separate markets.

There are several technical problems with the collection of the comparative price information which is the basis of the report. Most of the problems are acknowledged in the study. The main ones are:

1 Although the products surveyed are specifically defined, they still may not be comparable. For example, different

insurance premiums in the countries may reflect differences in underlying risk in the member states.
2 Cross-subsidization between financial products may often occur, which will obviously distort any figures.
3 The services surveyed may not have been representative of the financial sector as a whole, and the definitions of these services may not have been representative of each type of product.
4 Significant variations in price for products often occur between countries, and so the figures given may not have been representative of the institutions in each country.
5 Because relative prices change rapidly, the report only gives a 'snap-shot' of the situation at a certain point in time.

If the comparative price data in the report is accepted as an accurate reflection of practices there are still problems in converting it into expected price falls, and then into gains in consumer surplus. The weighting system used to calculate potential price falls was based on estimates of value added for each product, and the gains in consumer surplus were calculated using the estimated value added for the overall sectors. The measure of output used for the banking market was loans outstanding. However, there are several snags with this, because (the report rightly points out) this measure does not take into account some of the factors which affect banks' output. These include the number of off-balance sheet transactions, differences in risk attaching to loans, and the extent of deposit and money transmission services. It was also necessary to make estimates of elasticity of demand for financial services to change the price falls calculated into gains in consumer surplus. Because there was very little information on this available this estimate was based, almost entirely, on research on elasticity of demand in life insurance, and a uniform figure was assumed for each country.

Criticisms of the report

The study's results seem very encouraging, as they indicate that the integration of the financial services markets in the countries examined will bring substantial economic gains, especially in Britain. However, it has been argued that the results are both over-optimistic and unreliable. Certainly it would seem that, because of the many methodological problems just outlined, the results are liable to be subject to a big margin of error. To allow for this, the gains in consumer surplus have been based on a range of possible price falls rather than on exact figures.

However, it is also possible to criticize the report on the grounds that some of its assumptions seem to be arbitrary in the extreme. For example, it is assumed that potential price falls in a completely liberalized market would equal the average of the lowest four prices observed. This does not seem to have any theoretical base whatsoever. There are economic arguments to support the assumption that prices will fall, but it seems to be guesswork which has been used to determine by how much. It is also significant that, where the prices were below the average of the four lowest it was not assumed that any price increases would occur. If such increases did happen the results would be even more of an over-estimation. The study also allows for the fact that not all the elements which cause price differences will be removed by the integration of the markets in a totally arbitrary manner, i.e. by reducing the potential price falls by between 40 and 60 per cent to obtain the expected price falls. Finally, as the report itself says, the figures assume that there would be a competitive market structure after integration, while 'the realism of this assumption is open to question'.

Because of these criticisms, it has been argued that the price fall estimates could be subject to a far greater margin of error than that for which the report allows. Therefore, it is possible that the countries with the lowest expected price reductions could, instead, actually face price increases as cross-border demand for their products rose. This, of course, would mean that there would be losses rather than gains in consumer surplus. This may be too pessimistic a view, but it does show that the predicted gains for countries, including for the UK, are by no means certain to happen.

The expected gains in consumer surplus have also been questioned on the following grounds. The idea that prices will be reduced is based on the assumption that competition will greatly increase because of the single market programme.

There is no doubt that this will be so in the short term, but over the longer term it is possible that the internal market could actually reduce competition. The rise in mergers and acquisitions in the financial sector (and in every sector) will increase industry concentration. Extreme concentration could lead to an oligopolistic market, with a few huge institutions dominating the sector. However, in view of the barriers to large-scale mergers and acquisitions in the financial sector which are liable to remain even after 1992 (see pp. 85–6), this is unlikely to happen.

OTHER POSSIBLE SOURCES OF GAIN FROM THE INTEGRATION OF THE FINANCIAL SERVICES MARKETS

The Cecchini Report emphasizes the possible gains in consumer surplus that could arise because of reductions in prices as a result of 1992. However, other sources of economic gain from integrating the financial markets of Europe have also been predicted.

The first is reduced business costs, as a result of institutions being able to take advantage of economies of scale by expanding and diversifying their operations, and therefore lowering their unit costs. However, it is doubtful whether these economies of scale would occur. Many banks in Europe are very large and already conduct business abroad, before the market has been opened up, and so would already be benefiting from any available economies of scale. It is also uncertain whether or not economies of scale actually exist in the banking market. It has been suggested that, when an institution grows above a certain size, diseconomies rather than economies of scale may be more likely to occur. Gains in terms of wider consumer choice are also expected, because of customers' access to a larger number of banks and their products, and because of greater innovation by the banks as competition between them increases. Most of the microeconomic effects of the completion of the internal market in stimulating demand (see pp. 43–4) should also apply equally to banking as to other industries. Therefore, integrating the financial markets should lead to increased employment in the long term. On a wider level, integrated financial markets should benefit the Community's economy as a whole. The financial sector has an important role in assisting other industries, and so increased efficiency and lower prices in the financial markets will benefit all other European businesses.

ECONOMIC IMPLICATIONS OF LIBERALIZING THE CAPITAL MARKETS

The liberalization and integration of Europe's capital markets is expected to bring two specific benefits. First, access to a wider range of markets and investments will give greater opportunities for portfolio diversification. The more restricted investors are in the assets that they can hold in their portfolios, the worse their possible combinations of risk and return. It has been shown that the gains from such international diversification can be substantial – one study indicated returns almost 75 per cent higher than before.

The second benefit arises from the convergence of real interest rates. Exchange controls at present prevent capital from moving freely to those countries which offer the highest rates of return. When these controls are removed it is probable that some convergence of real interest rates will occur, which will help limit the distortions in capital flow which are bound to happen. The Cecchini Report provides a methodology to quantify the potential welfare gains resulting from the complete equalization of interest rates, but cautions that they would be small compared to the gains resulting from the reduced prices in the financial sector. This convergence will also be limited by a reluctance to borrow or invest in other countries for as long as exchange rates fluctuate. Therefore, even the small possible gains will not be fully realized.

POSSIBLE DISTORTIONS IN SAVINGS

A major division exists within the EC at present over the issues of withholding tax and bank secrecy. Currently these vary enormously from one member state to another and will have to be harmonized to prevent massive distortions in savings when capital controls are lifted. The rates of withholding tax in the Community vary from between 0 per cent and 50 per cent, and most of those states which do deduct tax at source from residents' savings exempt the savings of non-residents. In those countries which do not impose a withholding tax, banks are usually not required to inform the tax authorities of the amount of interest paid on savings. Thus, if this confused situation remains after 1992 wealthy individuals will be tempted to place their savings in any country but their own, leading to a large distortion of savings patterns.

One member state which is very concerned about this is France. At the moment it has one of the highest rates of withholding tax in the EC, and is afraid that these tax differences could precipitate large outflows of money and losses of tax revenue when exchange controls are removed (French residents are not allowed to hold bank accounts in other countries at present). For this reason, France has made taking measures 'for the removal or reduction of the risk of distortion, tax avoidance and evasion' arising from the differences in Community tax systems a precondition of lifting its exchange controls.

The Commission has set out proposals for the approximation of withholding taxes (or for the introduction of a minimum withholding tax at the very least) and for banks to be required to provide their tax authorities with details of interest paid on Community residents' savings. However, these proposals have been met with much opposition, mainly from the UK and Germany, but also from the Netherlands and Luxembourg. Britain is worried that such legislation would adversely affect London's position as a leading financial centre. Foreign deposits in the UK are currently exempt from the composite rate withholding tax to which residents' savings are subject, and therefore London attracts deposits from other Community countries where residents are also charged withholding tax, such as Belgium, Ireland and Italy. When exchange controls are abolished the UK will be able to attract deposits from those countries, like France, whose residents are not at present allowed to place their money abroad. However, these proposals on withholding taxes will greatly reduce London's ability to attract such deposits.

Opposition to the proposals has also come from those countries which have no withholding tax at present, or just a low rate, because any increases in the rate would be likely to lead to large outflows of capital from them. Germany recently introduced a withholding tax of 10 per cent and, according to Deutsche Bank, this led to an estimated DM 20 billion (approximately £6.3 billion) leaving the country in the first seven months of 1988. The German authorities were so alarmed by this that the tax was abandoned, and the Germans are extremely unwilling to reimpose a withholding tax again, regardless of the rate. Much of the money from Germany is thought to have gone to Luxembourg. The Grand Duchy acts as the EC's tax haven at present, with no withholding tax, no capital gains tax on collective investment funds and total bank secrecy; it is also unhappy about the Commission's proposals, as it benefits so much from the current tax differences.

Therefore, although the proposals are essential to prevent competitive distortions and loss of revenue through tax evasion, the EC is faced with a problem. If effective measures are introduced by it to try to prevent tax evasion the money which is currently deposited in the Community, but avoids tax because of the laws of the different countries, is liable simply to be moved to tax havens outside the Community, such as Switzerland. Therefore, any action could result in very large outflows of capital from the Community as a whole.

Apart from these problems, and the effect that the proposals will have on individual countries, some member states (and in particular the UK) are likely to oppose them on the grounds that taxation is a national matter, and handing any power over it to the EC represents a loss of national sovereignty. Taxation is one area where agreement on proposals still has to be unanimous, and so it is unlikely that a Community-wide withholding tax will be introduced in the foreseeable future. However, tax adjustments are frequently made in local markets without causing any major disruption, because what matters to investors in the end is the net amount of money they receive. This is determined more by absolute interest rates, rather than by minor differences in taxes.

ECONOMIC AND MONETARY UNION

Another issue relevant to the single financial market is the possibility of moves towards further monetary integration. In 1988 the European Commission set up a committee under the chairmanship of M. Jacques Delors to consider the actions which would be needed in order to establish full economic and monetary union within the EC. The committee presented its report in April 1989.

Complete economic and monetary union entails full freedom of movement for all goods, services, capital and people throughout the EC, the irrevocable fixing of exchange rates between national currencies, together with a common monetary policy for the participating states. A single, common currency is not an integral part of EMU, but it is a logical step. To create EMU within the EC the single market programme would have to be completed and complemented by action in three areas: there would have to be common policies to ensure the equitable allocation of resources in regions where market forces needed to be reinforced; there would have to be effective competition policies and other measures to strengthen market mechanisms; and there would need to be macro-economic co-ordination to create a Community-wide fiscal policy, for example in the area of national budgets.

EMU would give several benefits to the participating countries. It would reinforce the benefits of the single market, because fixed exchange rates would encourage greater cross-border trade and therefore greater competition and economies of scale. Fixed exchange rates should also lead to an optimum allocation of capital within the Community. If EMU also included a single, common currency, transaction costs incurred when currencies are exchanged for one another would be eliminated. Another benefit would be the saving of international reserves through their pooling. Because the sum of the reserves held by the member states independently is greater than the amount of pooled reserves which would have to be held, the countries would be able to enjoy a real resource advantage when running their reserves down to the new, lower level, by allowing exports to be exceeded by imports and running a higher temporary trade deficit than they are able to do currently while acting independently.

There are, of course, also disadvantages to EMU. Currently, if one member state suffers a faster rate of inflation than the others, devaluation is often used to curb it. This would not be possible under a system of irrevocably fixed exchange rates, and instead the country would incur at least some temporary unemployment. EMU would also mean that all the participating states would sacrifice some freedom to determine their own national economic policies.

Previous attempts at EMU

There have been attempts in the past to integrate the economic and monetary policies of the EC member states. These attempts have had varying degrees of success, depending upon the level of integration aimed at. The first attempt was in the early 1970s. In 1971 the member states expressed 'their political will to establish an economic and monetary union'. The motivation behind this move was a combination of the desire to help the working of the Common Agricultural Policy (which would have benefited from irrevocably fixed exchange rates), and to avoid large revaluations and devaluations of currencies.

As part of this integration process the 'snake in the tunnel' exchange rate mechanism was created in 1972. Under this, two bands of fluctuation between currencies were established. The wider band (the tunnel) was between each European currency and the US dollar. The permissible margin of fluctuation against the dollar was set at parity ±2.25 per cent, i.e. the maximum width of the band was 4.5 per cent. The width of the smaller band (the snake) between the currencies of participating states was 2.25 per cent, with a margin of fluctuation of parity ±1.125 per cent. The success of this snake mechanism was limited, with countries joining and floating out of it at regular intervals. The idea of EMU also floundered, partly because of the unsettled conditions of the international monetary system at the time, and partly because the EC member states did not co-ordinate their national economic and monetary policies.

The existing European Monetary System (EMS) was set up in 1979 in order to establish a European zone of monetary stability, to counter the destabilizing effect foreign currency movements were having (especially those of the US dollar), and to encourage investment and business. There are three main components of the EMS: the European Monetary Co-operation Fund (EMCF), the European Currency Unit (ECU), which is made up of a weighted basket of participating currencies, and the Exchange Rate Mechanism (ERM).

Under the ERM (or 'supersnake'), each currency has a central exchange rate fixed in terms of ECU. From this rate bilateral central exchange rates between each currency are calculated, from which a maximum fluctuation margin of 2.25 per cent is allowed (except for sterling and the Italian lira, which is allowed a 6 per cent fluctuation margin). To keep exchange rates within the permissible bands intervention from the appropriate Central Banks may be needed. For example, if the Danish kroner falls to its 2.25 per cent floor against the German deutschmark, the Danish Central Bank has to sell deutschmark while the Bundesbank buys kroner. The ERM is a flexible system, with both devaluation and revaluation allowed, although they have to be negotiated between the participating states. All the member states take part in the ERM, except Greece and Portugal.

The Delors Committee report

The Delors Committee report set out a three-stage plan for achieving full economic and monetary union, each stage leading on from the previous one. It was emphasized that the process was to be regarded as a continuous one, and that once member states had decided to embark upon Stage 1 of the plan they should be committed to following through the subsequent stages. No fixed timetable was set, although the committee made it clear that Stage 1 should start no later than 1 July 1990, when capital movements became fully liberalized.

Under Stage 1 of the plan, economic and monetary policy co-ordination would be strengthened using the institutional framework which already exists. The internal market (especially the internal financial market) would be completed and fully implemented. All the Community currencies would participate in the ERM, under the same rules; and the Committee of Central Bank Governors (CCBG) would be given new powers to formulate opinions on overall Community monetary and exchange rate policy, and to express opinions to individual governments and the Council of Ministers on policies that could affect the Community's monetary situation. The CCBG would also be consulted about national monetary policy. There would also be a new Procedure (replacing the 1974 Council Directive on Economic Convergence), which would establish a new process of budgetary co-ordination with precise, quantitative guidelines, would set up a process for multilateral surveillance of economic policies and developments based on agreed indicators, and would provide for co-ordinated budgetary actions by Community states.

Stage 2 of the plan could be implemented only after a new treaty was signed, as neither the original Treaty of Rome nor the Single European Act provide a legal basis for EMU. This would be a transition stage, with ultimate authority still residing with national bodies, but with the new institutional framework gradually taking over to promote common decision-making in the economic and monetary fields. The Community would set precise (but not yet binding) rules on the size of the member states' annual budget deficits and their financing, and would establish a medium-term framework of key economic objectives to achieve stable growth, together with procedures to monitor member states' performance and to correct any differences. A European System of Central Banks (ESCB) would also be set up, in order to form and implement monetary policy and to manage the EC's exchange rate policy with non-EC countries. The ESCB would consist of a central institution and the national Central Banks.

The final stage would see the irrevocable locking of exchange rates and the evolution of a single monetary policy. Responsibility for forming and implementing monetary policy would be transferred to the ESCB, and that body would pool and manage all official reserves. Community rules in the budgetary and macro-economic areas would become binding; for example, the Council of Ministers would have the power to impose constraints on national budgets if monetary stability was threatened. Preparations would also be made for the transition to a single currency.

The steps set out above would be accompanied by action on competition policy in the Community and by measures to ensure adequate and fair resource allocation throughout the regions of the EC.

At the Madrid Heads of Government summit in June 1989 all the member states accepted the principle of a step-by-step approach to EMU, and they confirmed that Stage 1 would begin by 1 July 1990. It was also decided to set up a special inter-government conference to discuss the changes needed to implement Stages 2 and 3.

Britain's position

Despite the agreement at Madrid, the UK in particular had a number of reservations about the Delors report and its approach to EMU. Its main criticisms were that the commitment to implementing Stages 2 and 3 of the plan before the results of the first stage were known was remarkably foolhardy (this view was shared by other countries as well); that binding rules on the size of budget deficits were unnecessary; that it was by no means certain that the ESCB would prove to be effective in implementing anti-inflationary policies, and that its power could only be balanced by a European finance ministry of a European central government – something no member state would accept; and that it would reduce national sovereignty by taking monetary policy out of the control of individual governments.

As an alternative to the Delors plan, Britain produced another plan for EMU in November 1989, entitled *An Evolutionary Approach to Economic and Monetary Union*, building on Stage 1 of the Delors approach. Its advantages were felt to be that it advocated a multi-currency system, which would lead to a convergence of inflation rates because of competition between monetary authorities; a system of fixed exchange rates would evolve; it would allow monetary policy to remain the preserve of national governments, but at the same time within a framework of improved co-operation; and it would not involve any major constitutional changes. The Chancellor, John Major, summed them up:

> The merit of our approach is that it is evolutionary . . . . It is also robust. More robust than the Delors approach, which courts great risks, needlessly, by proposing that decisions should be taken on the next stage of the process before we have had a chance to assess the outcome of the first stage.

Britain's proposals were considered by the European Council at Strasbourg in December 1989, but were rejected. Therefore the UK is committed to abiding by the Delors plan.

The threat to national sovereignty still remains, although the Delors report emphasized that as much decision-making power as possible would be kept by the various national authorities. But it is debatable how much national sovereignty over economic policy countries still retain, when even informal economic integration reduces the ability of member states to pursue independent policies.

Chapter 8
Conclusions

The single market programme started in 1985 is, without doubt, the most comprehensive and wide-ranging attempt yet to create a true internal market in the EC, encompassing all sections of the economy. All the member states and all types of businesses are set to benefit substantially from this programme. The financial services market should benefit especially, as previous progress in the removal of barriers to the free provision of services has been much slower than for the removal of barriers to the free provision of goods. Chapter 1 demonstrated the importance of the financial market to the Community's economy, in terms both of its size and of its effect on other industries. The gains resulting from the integration of the financial markets predicted by the Cecchini Report are among the largest of any individual sector examined, totalling approximately 0.75 per cent of gross domestic product. However, it remains to be seen whether or not these predicted gains will materialize fully.

THE IMPORTANCE OF THE BANKING LEGISLATION

The Community's banking legislation will affect banks in three main ways: they will be able to open branches throughout the Community without having to meet the host countries' authorization requirements, and with far less bureaucracy than at present; they will be able to provide the entire range of services that they do in their home countries in the other member states; and, with the removal of exchange controls, banks will be able to provide cross-border services without any restrictions. The great majority of the existing regulatory barriers will be removed by the legislation, together with the bureaucracy which faces banks at present. Some barriers, however, will still remain, in the form of host country control over certain matters.

However, few overt regulatory barriers actually exist in the financial market, although restrictions in the highly regulated member states can pose problems to banks wanting to expand their operations into those countries. The British Banking Association summed up the situation thus: 'We are concerned here with the removal of irritants rather than the creation of whole new opportunities.' The main exception is the presence of exchange controls, which are an insuperable barrier to a free financial market in some countries. In general, though, the Community's legislation will not create radical new opportunites for banks, although it will greatly help their expansion into other member states.

The indirect effect on banks of 1992 (i.e. the effect the single market has on banks' customers) may well turn out to be more profound than the direct effect of the banking legislation. The changes that banks will have to make to serve the new needs of their customers after 1992 should not be forgotten or underestimated.

THE PROSPECTS FOR BRITISH BANKS

The effects of 1992 will not be evenly spread across the Community. The countries which are currently the most regulated and the least open to foreign competition will be the most affected. Probably the greatest effects will be felt in Spain, where tight restrictions on foreign entrants to the market and domestic bank inefficiency have resulted in the country being one of the most expensive in Europe for bank products. The high profit margins which the home banks earn also mean that there is likely to be a rush of foreign banks into Spain when restrictions are lifted.

In contrast, the increase in competition in the UK banking market will not be nearly so noticeable. This is for a number of reasons. First, the UK already has one of the most open markets in the EC, with no exchange controls, no restrictions on the activities foreign banks can undertake, and no branch endowment capital requirements. Second, competition in the UK financial market is already fairly fierce. The institutions are efficient, and there are no abnormal profit margins to attract foreign banks. Finally, all the major banking institutions (both from the EC and from third countries) are already established in London, although institutions from highly regulated countries may offer more competition when the restrictions on their operations are removed (especially as many of them are more capitalized than the UK banks if debt provisions for developing countries are taken into account). Therefore, as far as traditional banking activities are concerned, deregulation will give UK banks significant opportunities to expand their operations into new markets, but will probably not pose too much of a threat to their domestic market.

The picture is not so bright for the UK securities market, however, because of the recent Financial Services Act. This imposes quite strict restrictions on UK operators in the securities business, and, because of the principle of home country control, foreign players will be exempt from its provisions. This will put British banks at a distinct disadvantage to foreign institutions in the securities business, both in the UK market and abroad. If its effects are too severe, however, it is possible that the Act may be modified.

In general, the single market presents more opportunities than threats to British institutions, and they tend to be well-placed to meet its challenges and to take full advantage of the benefits available from it.

THE CHANGES IN COMMUNITY BANKING

A large amount of restructuring has been going on among Community banks and institutions, and doubtless this will continue. However, this has not altered the look of European banking to any great extent, as in the majority of the mergers and acquisitions which have taken place at least one party has been a comparatively small institution. It does seem fairly unlikely that European banking will come to be controlled by just a few 'super-banks', due to the size and diversity of the present market.

In retail banking, because of the enormous costs involved in setting up or acquiring a branch network, the emphasis after 1992 is likely to shift away from branching to less conventional methods of distributing financial products and services. Technology will be increasingly used to develop and provide new services. Home and telephone banking are likely to become more and more common, and plastic cards (which are ideal for cross-border transactions) will become much more sophisticated, being used to deliver many kinds of financial services instead of acting merely as credit and debit cards. This change in delivery systems will, in turn, influence the types of services most commonly offered. There will be less competition among the banks to offer those services which still need to be sold through branch networks than for those which do not.

For those banks which do wish to establish significant physical market presences in other member states, mergers and acquisitions have been very popular for this, and will continue to be used in preference to the prohibitively expensive green-fields approach. Probably the best method of gaining access to foreign customers is through co-operative business links, and many more of these strategic alliances can be expected in the future.

A TRUE SINGLE MARKET IN BANKING?

To examine whether or not 1992 will create a true, free internal market in banking it is necessary to distinguish between the retail and wholesale sides of the industry. The single market programme will remove practically all the regulatory barriers preventing a free European banking market. However, in retail banking, even in those countries like the UK, where the market has been completely open to foreign banks for over a decade, many aspects of banking have remained predominantly national concerns. This is because there are many unofficial barriers, and these have perhaps even more of an effect in restricting foreign banks from entering markets than do official barriers. The most important of these unofficial barriers are the huge costs of establishing a market presence, the problems of changing local customs and habits, and people's preference for familiar names and institutions. These barriers cannot be legislated away, and will prevent a true single market in retail banking being created after 1992 (although there will be an increase in competition).

Unlike retail banking, the wholesale sector is already very internationalized, and on a global scale rather than just a European one. The unofficial barriers which restrict retail banking do not apply here, and it is really only exchange controls which have hampered the complete internationalization of wholesale banking. When these have all finally been removed there will be virtually no obstacles, official or unofficial, preventing the development of a free internal market in corporate banking. However, for those countries which have already removed all exchange controls, the single market programme will have very little noticeable effect in this sector. Because of the global nature of corporate banking it will also be just as easy for EC banks to conduct business in non-EC countries as it will be to do so in other member states.

THE EFFECT ON LONDON

The emphasis the single market programme has on home country control will mean that banks will prefer to base themselves in the member state with the least restrictive supervisory regime. This could lead to some institutions relocating to other countries. Until recently, the most obvious financial centre for these banks to choose to relocate to was London, and it probably still is for institutions undertaking traditional banking activities only. However, banks increasingly are becoming involved in the securities business, and as securities trading is covered by the single licence of the Second Banking Co-ordination Directive, this trend towards universal banking will probably continue and grow. The UK Financial Services Act means that London is now one of the most regulated European centres for securities trading. This fact may attract foreign investors who feel that they are not well enough protected in their domestic markets, but it may also lead to third-country banks basing their subsidiaries in less regulated financial centres. London could lose a significant amount of business because of this.

This raises the possibility of other European financial centres, such as Paris or Frankfurt, developing to offer serious competition to London in the single market. London owes its position as the main financial centre of Europe partly because of its open, deregulated markets. Because of the Financial Services Act (and, to a lesser extent, the recent Banking Act) it is, however, loosing this reputation. As other European centres will become far less regulated after 1992 there have been some fears about London's ability to maintain its pre-eminence.

London does, however, have several other advantages over its rivals in addition to its open markets. The main advantage is the sheer size of its financial markets, and the wealth of capital and expertise that is concentrated there. Financial services tend to generate a bandwagon effect: business flows to the largest market. Another advantage London has is its domination of the time zones in the global marketplace. Because of these reasons, and because of the relatively low tax rates in the UK and the practice of universal banking, London's position in Europe will probably not be seriously threatened.

As a final point, it should be noted that the idea of international financial integration is not something new. The single market's effect will be to accelerate a trend towards the internationalization of financial markets which has been going on for a number of years. This wider dimension of 1992 must not be ignored. It is very important that the European market remains open to the rest of the world and fulfils a global role, and that its aim is the further integration of the world markets.

Appendix I

Table AI.1 European top 50 banks by capital, 1988

Rank		Capital ($ million)	Assets ($ million)	
1	National Westminster, London	10,907	178,505	5
2	Barclays, London	10,545	189,368	3
3	Crédit Agricole, Paris	9,152	210,601	1
4	Union Bank of Switzerland	6,715	110,760	11
5	Deutsche Bank, Frankfurt	6,460	170,808	6
6	Swiss Bank Corporation, Basle	6,055	102,466	13
7	Lloyds Bank, London	5,867	93,800	17
8	Banque Nationale de Paris	5,567	196,955	2
9	Midland Bank, London	5,499	100,849	15
10	Crédit Lyonnaise, Paris	5,409	178,878	4
11	Paribas, Paris	5,324	121,617	10
12	Société Générale, Paris	4,874	145,661	8
13	Crédit Suisse, Zurich	4,785	75,388	24
14	Rabobank, Utrecht	4,666	80,808	22
15	Group Ecureuil, Paris	4,372	150,253	7
16	Dresdner Bank, Frankfurt	4,284	129,733	9
17	Banco Bilbao Vizcaya	4,138	63,340	28
18	Instituto Bancario S. Paolo	4,075	103,105	12
19	Monte di Paschi di Siena	3,625	66,560	27
20	Cariplo, Milan	3,504	54,131	38
21	SE Banken, Stockholm	3,412	46,965	40
22	TSB Group, London	3,364	40,078	49
23	Banca Naz del Lavoro, Rome	3,352	87,729	19
24	Banco Central, Madrid	3,200	40,659	46
25	Banca Comm. Italiana, Milan	3,178	62,700	30
26	Commerzbank, Frankfurt	3,133	101,331	14
27	Algemene Bank Ned'land	3,130	85,176	20

Rank		Capital ($ million)	Assets ($ million)	
28	Amro Bank, Amsterdam	2,961	84,072	21
29	Istituto Mobiliare Italiano	2,940	23,836	75
30	West LB Bank, Dusseldorf	2,568	96,147	16
31	Union Bank of Finland	2,542	31,810	62
32	Svenska Handelsbanken	2,510	38,658	54
33	Banco Espanol de Credito	2,332	27,385	68
34	Credito Italiano, Milan	2,319	56,952	34
35	Bayerische Vereinsbank	2,280	91,244	18
36	Kredit W'aufbau, Frankfurt	2,188	54,467	37
37	Standard Chartered, London	2,166	42,874	44
38	Royal Bank of Scotland	2,152	36,508	59
39	Groupe des Banques Pop.	2,143	56,124	35
40	Bayerische-Hypo & Weschsel	2,101	75,927	23
41	PKbanken, Stockholm	2,045	39,588	50
42	Compagnie Bancaire, Paris	2,000	30,737	64
43	Den Danske Bank	1,883	23,339	77
44	Bayerische Landesbank	1,717	71,914	26
45	Banco Santander, Santander	1,703	29,462	65
46	Creditanstalt-Bankverein	1,695	39,041	51
47	DG Bank, Frankfurt	1,647	74,009	25
48	Générale Bank, Brussels	1,601	61,954	31
49	Banque Indosuez, Paris	1,539	48,156	39
50	CIC Group, Paris	1,509	63,021	29

Source: *The Banker*, October 1989

Table AI.2 European top 300 banks by country

Rank		Capital ($ million)		Assets ($ million)	
Belgium					
48	Générale Bank, Brussels	1,601	1	61,954	1
65	ASLK-CGER Bank, Brussels	1,233	2	40,168	4
69	Kreditbank, Brussels	1,108	3	38,849	5
76	Bank B. Lambert, Brussels	953	4	45,293	2
79	Crédit Comm. Belg., Brussels	929	5	40,251	3
111	Cera Spaarbank, Leuven	651	6	13,194	7
135	Bacob Savings Bank, Brussels	522	7	11,405	8
188	An-Hyp, Antwerp	340	8	5,430	9
194	Soc. Nationale, Brussels	330	9	15,731	6
Denmark					
43	Den Danske, Copenhagen	1,883	1	23,339	1

Appendix I

Rank		Capital ($ million)		Assets ($ million)	
72	C'hagen Handels, C'hagen	1,056	2	17,995	3
77	BRF Bygg Realkredit, Lyngby	934	3	18,202	2
89	Sparekassen SDS, C'hagen	852	4	14,846	5
90	Privatbanken, C'hagen	852	5	14,920	4
117	Bikuben, C'hagen	604	6	8,790	7
122	Provinsbanken, Arhus	581	7	9,306	6
133	Andelsbanken, C'hagen	543	8	8,217	8
141	Jykse Bank, C'hagen	493	9	7,729	9
254	Sparekassen, Nord., Aalborg	215	10	3,264	11
281	Sydbank, Aabenraa	192	11	3,342	10
294	Sparekassen Sydjylland, Vejle	181	12	2,782	12

Republic of Ireland

63	Bank of Ireland, Dublin	1,254	1	15,626	2
88	Allied Irish Banks, Dublin	853	2	20,736	1

France

3	Crédit Agricole, Paris	9,152	1	210,601	1
8	Banque Nationale, Paris	5,567	2	196,955	2
10	Crédit Lyonnaise, Paris	5,409	3	178,878	3
11	Paribas, Paris	5,324	4	121,617	6
12	Société Générale, Paris	4,874	5	145,661	5
15	Group Ecureuil, Paris	4,372	6	150,253	4
39	Groupe des Banques, Paris	2,143	7	56,124	8
42	Compagnie Bancaire, Paris	2,000	8	30,737	12
49	Banque Indosuez, Paris	1,539	9	48,156	9
50	CIC Group, Paris	1,509	10	63,021	7
59	Crédit Comm. de France, Paris	1,310	11	38,515	10
123	Crédit du Nord, Paris	573	12	19,965	13
125	Sovac, Paris	563	13	6,897	19
130	Al Ubaf Banking Group, Paris	548	14	13,401	14
214	Cie Parisienne Rees., Paris	267	15	7,465	17
220	Féd. du Crédit, Strasbourg	257	16	7,164	18
251	Banque Worms, Paris	221	17	10,192	15
265	Banque Sudameris, Paris	206	18	5,644	22
273	BFCE, Paris	199	19	38,281	11
282	Eurobank, Paris	191	20	6,373	20
297	Société de Thomson, Paris	177	21	2,604	26

West Germany

5	Deutsche Bank, Frankfurt	6,460	1	170,808	1
16	Dresdner Bank, Frankfurt	4,284	2	129,733	2
26	Commerzbank, Frankfurt	3,133	3	101,331	3
30	West LB Bank, Dusseldorf	2,568	4	96,147	4
35	Bayerische Vereins., Munich	2,280	5	91,244	5
36	Kredit W'aufbau, Frankfurt	2,188	6	54,467	10
40	Bayerische Hypo., Munich	2,101	7	75,927	6
44	Bayerische Landes, Munich	1,717	8	71,914	8
47	DG Bank, Frankfurt	1,647	9	74,009	7
57	Norddeutsche L'bank, Hanover	1,381	10	60,557	9

Rank		Capital ($ million)		Assets ($ million)	
60	BFG Bank, Frankfurt	1,304	11	37,440	14
70	LB Baden-Wurtte., Stuttgart	1,101	12	23,984	18
78	Wohnungsbau-Kredit, Berlin	930	13	13,380	30
92	Hessische L'bank, Frankfurt	835	14	38,865	13
96	BHF Bank, Frankfurt	811	15	18,834	23
102	Hamburger Spark, Hamburg	740	16	15,065	27
104	SWdeutsche L'bank, Stuttgart	730	17	40,723	12
108	Deutsch Pfand., Wiesbaden	668	18	43,390	11
110	L'bank Rheinland-Pfalz, Mainz	658	19	24,321	17
112	WD Genossen., Dusseldorf	648	20	16,024	26
114	Hamburgische, Hamburg	623	21	25,191	16
115	SGZ Bank, Frankfurt	608	22	14,187	28
137	Landw'liche Renten, Frankfurt	508	23	17,668	24
143	Industriekredit, Dusseldorf	483	24	12,159	31
145	Landesgirokässe, Stuttgart	480	25	10,873	35
146	Berliner Bank, Berlin	479	26	18,918	22
150	Sparkässe der Stadt, Berlin	454	27	12,059	32
155	Deutsche Giro, Frankfurt	438	28	23,446	19
157	Bayerische Landes., Munich	425	29	8,802	38
159	LB Schleswig-Holstein, Kiel	415	30	19,017	21
164	Vereins & W'bank, Hamburg	404	31	11,184	33
172	ND Genossen., Hanover	383	32	9,724	36
176	Bankhaus W. Werhahn, Neuss	365	33	1,363	107
178	Genossenschaftliche, Stuttgart	363	34	11,077	34
179	DSL Bank, Bonn	361	35	25,218	15
195	Bremer Landesbank, Bremen	326	36	17,110	25
197	Stadtsparkässe Koln, Cologne	318	37	8,976	37
202	Kreissparkässe Koln, Cologne	305	38	6,580	46
205	Stadtspark. München, Munich	296	39	6,875	45
207	Baden-Württemberg, Stuttgart	289	40	7,423	42
218	Sparkässe in Bremen, Bremen	260	41	5,982	47
232	Sal. Oppenheim, Cologne	247	42	7,684	41
234	Frankfurter S.kässe, Frankfurt	243	43	5,790	48
239	Wohnungsbau Sch-Hol, Kiel	238	44	3,680	61
250	Nassauische S.kässe, W'baden	221	45	7,256	43
264	Deutsche Ausgleichs., Bonn	207	46	7,978	40
266	Deutsche Apotheker, Dusseldorf	206	47	5,335	51
275	Oldenburgische Landesbank	198	48	3,402	67
276	Allgemeine Hypo, Frankfurt	197	49	7,129	44
277	VAG Kredit, Braunschweig	197	50	2,089	95
284	Stadt-S'kässe, Dusseldorf	191	51	5,140	52
287	Stadtsparkässe, Dortmund	187	52	3,735	60
288	Sparkässe Essen, Essen	186	53	4,243	55
293	Berliner Pfandbrief-Bank	182	54	5,387	50
299	Landessparkässe Oldenburg	176	55	3,970	57

Greece

107	National Bank, Athens	677	1	26,125	1
140	Agricultural Bank, Athens	493	2	6,857	2
152	Hellenic Ind. Dev., Athens	443	3	2,535	6

Rank		Capital ($ million)		Assets ($ million)	
247	Commercial Bank, Athens	225	4	6,227	3
Italy					
18	Istituto Bancario, Turin	4,075	1	103,105	1
19	Monte dei Pasche di Siena	3,625	2	66,560	3
20	Cariplo, Milan	3,504	3	54,131	8
23	Banca Naz. del Lavoro, Rome	3,352	4	87,729	2
25	Banco Comm. Italiana, Milan	3,178	5	62,700	4
29	Istituto Mobiliare, Rome	2,940	6	23,836	10
34	Credito Italiano, Milan	2,319	7	56,952	6
51	Banco di Sicilia, Palermo	1,480	8	31,140	9
61	Crediop, Rome	1,283	9	18,694	16
62	Banco di Roma, Rome	1,263	10	54,757	7
67	Banca Popolare di Novara	1,169	11	23,016	11
73	Mediobanca, Milan	1,034	12	9,899	22
75	Banca Popolare di Milano	963	13	19,915	14
80	Banco di Napoli, Naples	919	14	57,394	5
81	Banco di Santo Spirito, Rome	917	15	19,010	15
91	Nuovo Ambrosiano, Rome	851	16	17,917	17
93	Credito Romagnolo, Bologna	817	17	11,700	19
95	Cassa di Torino, Turin	814	18	16,688	18
99	Naz de'Agricoltura, Rome	754	19	22,813	12
100	Cassa di Verona V & B, Verona	754	20	10,571	21
101	Banca Pop. di Verona, Verona	741	21	5,421	35
103	Cassa di Roma, Rome	735	22	20,648	13
118	Cassa di Calabria, Cosenza	603	23	6,208	31
124	Banca Pop. di Bergamo	569	24	8,388	25
127	Istituto di Credito, Rome	552	25	10,978	20
136	Banco di Sardegna, Sassari	517	26	5,761	34
148	Cassa di Bologna, Bologna	456	27	5,949	32
154	Credito Bergamasco	440	28	4,117	40
156	Agricola Mantovana, Mantua	433	29	3,835	42
160	Banca Popolare di Pordenone	412	30	1,506	81
163	Efibanca, Rome	405	31	6,420	30
169	Cattolica Veneto, Vicenza	396	32	8,881	24
170	Cassa di Pad. & Rov., Padua	395	33	7,153	27
171	Centrobanca, Milan	392	34	6,992	28
175	Pop. dell'Emilia, Modena	372	35	4,776	36
180	Piccolo C.Valt'ese, Sondrio	358	36	2,015	73
181	Cassa di Venezia, Venezia	357	37	3,429	49
184	Banca Pop. di Sondrio, Sondrio	347	38	2,495	61
186	Banca Popolare di Lecco, Lecco	342	39	3,626	46
190	Cassa di Cuneo, Cuneo	337	40	2,341	66
191	Banca San Geminiano, Modena	335	41	4,257	37
192	Cassa di Genova & Imperia	335	42	6,483	29
193	Banca Popolare Vicentina	331	43	2,386	63
198	Cassa di Udine & Pordenone	315	44	1,570	79
209	Pop. Comm. & Industria, Milan	274	45	3,313	50
210	Banco Popolare Veneta, Padua	271	46	3,797	43
211	Antoniana di P&T, Padua	269	47	4,147	39

Rank		Capital ($ million)		Assets ($ million)	
212	Cassa di Modena, Modena	269	48	2,646	57
219	Banco di Desio & D.Briaza	260	49	1,569	80
221	Banco Pop. di Ancona, Jesi	257	50	2,155	71
228	Cassa di Pistoia & Pescia	249	51	2,295	67
229	Cassa di Spezia, La Spezia	249	52	1,473	83
230	Cassa di Firenze, Florence	248	53	8,040	26
233	Banca del Fruili, Udine	245	54	3,439	48
235	Cassa di Parma, Parma	243	55	3,039	52
240	Banca Sicula, Trapani	237	56	1,151	94
242	Banca Pop. di Brescia, Brescia	232	57	1,896	75
243	Sicilcassa, Palermo	230	58	9,270	23
248	Banca San Paolo, Brescia	224	59	5,799	33
249	Cassa di Peggio Emilia	222	60	1,748	77
253	Banca Popolare di Lodi	217	61	3,014	53
261	Cassa di Prato, Prato	209	62	3,645	45
271	Banca Cred. Agrario, Brescia	201	63	3,586	47
272	Banca Monte Bologna & R	200	64	2,683	56
278	Cassa di Ravenna, Ravenna	195	65	1,018	99
279	Cassa di Ferrara, Ferrara	195	66	1,175	92
280	Cassa di Biella, Biella	194	67	1,764	76
295	Banca Popolare di Sassari	180	68	1,158	93
Luxembourg					
83	BCCI Holdings, Luxembourg	886	1	20,638	1
201	Caisse d'Espargne, Luxembourg	311	2	8,965	4
226	Banque Générale de Luxembourg	252	3	10,311	3
244	Banque Int. à Luxembourg	229	4	11,476	2
252	BAII Group, Luxembourg	218	5	5,394	6
289	Kredietbank Luxembourgeoise	185	6	8,371	5
The Netherlands					
14	Rabobank, Utrecht	4,666	1	80,808	3
27	ABN, Amsterdam	3,130	2	85,176	1
28	Amro Bank, Amsterdam	2,961	3	84,072	2
56	NMB Bank, Amsterdam	1,390	4	43,307	4
66	Postbank, Amsterdam	1,176	5	34,103	5
106	Verenigde Spaarbank, Utrecht	685	6	6,865	6
Portugal					
94	Caixa Geral, Lisbon	815	1	15,615	1
216	Banco Commerial, Lisbon	266	2	2,020	9
298	Banco Nac. Ultramarino, Lisbon	176	3	3,888	6
Spain					
17	Banco Bilbao Vizcaya	4,138	1	63,340	1
24	Banco Central, Madrid	3,200	2	40,659	2
33	Espanol de Credito, Madrid	2,332	3	27,385	6
45	Banco Santander, Santander	1,703	4	29,462	3
52	Hispano Americano, Madrid	1,451	5	27,772	5
55	Caja de Madrid, Madrid	1,406	6	15,306	9

Appendix I

Rank		Capital ($ million)		Assets ($ million)	
68	Popular Espanol, Madrid	1,120	7	17,889	8
74	La Caixa, Barcelona	1,022	8	28,128	4
109	Banco Ext. de Espana, Madrid	663	9	18,366	7
134	Caja de Catalunya, Barcelona	529	10	5,999	15
161	Bankinter, Madrid	412	11	6,946	12
165	Banco de Sabadell, Sabadell	403	12	6,389	13
177	Caja de Med., Alicante	363	13	4,377	21
183	Caja de Barcelona, Barcelona	347	14	9,627	11
199	Banca Catalana, Barcelona	313	15	6,378	14
208	Caja Lab. Pop., Guipuzcoa	278	16	2,225	30
225	Caja de Guipuzcoa, San Seb.	253	17	2,936	26
236	Banco Cred. Agricola, Madrid	241	18	5,004	18
241	Banco Pastor, Corunna	236	19	5,345	17
260	Caja de Ahorros de Zaragoza	210	20	5,504	16
262	Banco Guipuzcoano, San Seb.	209	21	3,129	23
267	Banco de Andalucia, Jerez	205	22	1,956	34
268	Caja de Galicia, Madrid	205	23	4,914	19
296	Banco de Fomento, Madrid	179	24	2,425	29
United Kingdom					
1	Nat Westminster Bank, London	10,907	1	178,505	2
2	Barclays, London	10,545	2	189,368	1
7	Lloyds Bank, London	5,867	3	93,800	4
9	Midland Bank, London	5,499	4	100,849	3
22	TSB Group, London	3,364	5	40,078	6
37	Standard Chartered, London	2,166	6	42,874	5
38	Royal Bank of Scotland, Edinburgh	2,152	7	36,508	7
53	Bank of Scotland, Edinburgh	1,446	8	24,483	8
71	S.G. Warburg Group, London	1,098	9	21,803	9
84	Kleinwort Benson, London	878	10	16,211	10
113	Morgan Grenfell, London	624	11	10,338	11
132	Yorkshire Bank, Leeds	543	12	5,764	15
139	Hambros, London	494	13	6,276	13
147	Schroders, London	461	14	4,839	18
173	Barings, London	376	15	4,622	19
182	Singer & F'lander, London	349	16	1,115	32
189	Saudi International, London	340	17	4,620	20
206	Moscow Narodny, London	292	18	3,756	22
213	Libra Bank, London	268	19	2,481	26
246	NM Rothschild, London	226	20	5,904	14
255	Scandinavian Bank, London	215	21	5,626	16
258	United Bank of Kuwait, London	212	22	4,157	21

Source: The Banker, October 1989

Appendix II

Table AII.1 Standard financial products surveyed for Cecchini Report

Banking services
1 Consumer credit — Annual cost of consumer loan of 500 ECU. Excess interest rate over money market rates.
2 Credit cards — Annual cost, assuming 500 ECU debit. Excess interest rate over money market rates.
3 Mortgages — Annual cost of home loan of 25,000 ECU. Excess interest rate over money market rates.
4 Travellers cheques — Cost for a private consumer of buying 500 ECU worth of travellers cheques.
5 Letters of credit — Cost of letter of credit of 50,000 ECU for three months.
6 Foreign exchange drafts — Cost to large corporate client of buying a commercial draft for 30,000 ECU.
7 Commercial loans — Annual cost (including commission and charges) of a commercial loan of 250,000 ECU to a medium-sized company.

Brokerage services
1 Private equity deals — Commission costs of cash bargain of 1,440 ECU.
2 Private gilt deals — Commission costs of cash bargain of 14,000 ECU.
3 Institutional equity deals — Commission costs of cash bargain of 288,000 ECU.
4 Institutional gilt deals — Commission costs of cash bargain of 7.2 million ECU.

Insurance services
1 Life insurance — Average annual cost of term (life) insurance.
2 Home insurance — Annual cost of fire and theft cover for house valued at 70,000 ECU and contents at 28,000 ECU.
3 Motor insurance — Annual cost of comprehensive insurance for driver of ten years' experience with no-claims bonus and 1.6 litre car.
4 Commercial fire and theft — Annual cover for premises valued at 387,240 ECU and stock at 232,344 ECU.

| 5 Public liability cover | Annual premium for engineering firm with 20 employees and an annual turnover of 1.29 million ECU. |

Source: The Cost of Non-Europe in Financial Services, Price Waterhouse.

Index

Abbey Life company 3, 98
Abbey National 98
accepting houses 2
African Caribbean Pacific
  countries 42
Agricultural Bank of Greece 12
Allianz 88
Allied Irish Bank 13–14
Allied Irish Securities 14
Amev 89
Amsterdam-Rotterdam Bank 88
Argentina 87
ASLK-CGER 5
automated teller machines 9, 14,
  92, 96; script ATM 14

Banca Credit West e dei Comuni
  Vesuviani 94
Banca d'America & d'Italia 16, 87
Banco Bilbao Vizcaya 88–9 96
Banco Co-operativo Espanol 89
Banco d'Asturias 94
Banco de Bilbao 21, 89
Banco de Comercio e Industria 96
Banco de Vizcaya 21, 89
Banco Nat West March 94
Banco Portugês do Atlântico 20
Banco Santander 95–6
Banco Totta & Acores 20
Banking Act 121
Banking Advisory Committee 71
banking licence 10, 50, 62; single
  banking licence 59–61, 75, 82, 120
Bank of America 87
Bank of England 60, 85
Bank of Ireland 13–14
Bank of Scotland 1, 92
banks: clearing 1–2, 13;
  commercial 4–8, 10–11, 15,
  18–22, 49–50, 54, 60, 80;
  consortium 3; co-operative 8,
  10, 15, 18, 70, 85, 89; merchant
  1–2, 7, 16, 60, 87, 96–8; mutual
  8, 85; regional 7, 10; rural 89;
  savings 4–6, 8–11, 15, 18–19,
  21–23, 54, 89
Banque Bruxelles Lambert 5
Banque Crédit Commercial 88
Banque de l'Union Européene 94
Banque National de Paris 8, 89
Barclays Bank 1, 86, 92, 94–5, 97
Barclays de Zeote Wedd 97–8
barriers: fiscal 34, 37–9, 47; non-
  regulatory 54–5, 81, 119–20;
  physical 34–5, 43, 47;
  regulatory 47–54, 67, 77, 85–6,
  100, 117, 119–20; technical
  34–7, 43, 47
Basle agreement on capital
  adequacy 72
Bayerische Hypotheken- &
  Wechel-Bank 88
Bayerische Kommunala
  Landesbank 89
Bayerische Vereinsbank 96
Belgium 18, 23, 28, 49, 53, 72, 81,
  83, 88, 95–6, 99, 108; banking
  system 4–6; monetary
  association with Luxembourg
  17, 53

Index

bills of exchange 90
bonds 3, 6–7, 10–11, 51–2; Eurobond market 18, 78; government bonds 7, 15, 21–2; mortgage bonds 7, 11, 19
branches 2, 5, 8, 10–11, 14–16, 21–2, 25, 47–50, 54, 56, 59, 61, 63–7, 73–6, 78, 80, 82, 84, 86–90, 93–5, 116, 118–19; green fields/organic branch growth 84–6, 93, 119
British Banking Association 67–8, 117
brokers, brokerage 3, 6–9, 13–15, 50, 75, 94, 96–8; broking system 6; commission 9, 22
budget deficit 113–14
building societies 2–3, 14, 81, 98; Building Societies Act (1986) 2
business links 84, 86–90, 92–6, 119

Canada 72
capital markets 20, 107; primary markets 4; secondary markets 4, 12
capital requirements 8, 46, 75, 118; minimum capital requirements 17, 22, 49, 61–2, 67, 72
Cazanove & Co 98
Cecchini, Paolo 44–5, 99
Cecchini Report 24, 44, 80–1, 83, 99–107, 116, criticisms of 104–6; methodological problems 103–4
certificates of deposit 9, 21, 75
Chase Manhattan 88
cheques 79
Commercial Bank of Greece 12
commercial paper 9; eurocommercial paper 75
Commercial Union 3
Commerzbank 10–11, 88
Committee of central bank governors 112
common market 27, 30, 32–5
Commonwealth 40
Community competition policy 45, 110, 113
Community legislation 29, 34, 58, 117; legislative process 31–3, 39; types of legislation 31–2
Compagnie Bancaire 80, 88
consumer credit 80–1, 83, 100
Consumer Credit Act 68
consumer surplus, gains in 99, 101–6; losses in 105
controls on capital movements *see* foreign exchange controls
Cornhill Insurance 88
corporate finance 20, 88, 96
Council of Ministers 28, 30–2, 39, 75, 112–13; role and responsibilities 29
Court of Auditors 31
Crédit Agricôle 8
credit cards 2, 9, 11, 16, 79, 83, 95, 119; Amex 11, 92; Carta Si 16; debit cards 11, 119; Eurocheque cards 11; Mastercard 9, 11, 16, 92; plastic cards 92, 97, 119; Visa 9, 11, 16, 92
credit institutions 6–7, 46–7, 56, 58–63, 65, 68, 70–8, 82; public credit institutions 4–5; specialised credit institutions 10, 16, 20
Crédit Lyonnaise 8, 87–8
cross-border trading 84, 95, 110, 119
cultural regions 83

Delors Committee report 112–15
Delors, Jaques 110
Denmark 11, 18, 23, 28, 42, 53, 80, 83, 96, 112; banking system 6–8; kroner 112
deregulation 46, 50, 53, 60, 100, 118, 121
Deutsche Bank 10–11, 83, 87–8, 94, 109
Deutsche Terminborse 12
devaluation 110–12
DG Bank 89
directive on the accounts of foreign branches 56, 74–5

directive on the annual accounts of credit institutions 56, 74–5
directive on consolidated supervision 47
directive on investment services in the securities field 75, 82
directive removing controls on capital movements 52, 57
directive on the reorganization and winding up of credit institutions 56, 74
Dresdner Bank 10–11, 88–90
Dublin 15; off-shore financial centre 15

economic and monetary union 109–115; 'an evolutionary approach to economic and monetary union' 114
Economic and Social Committee 30–1
economic convergence directive 113
economies of scale 36, 43–4, 106, 110
elasticity of demand 101, 104
equity 3, 6–7, 12, 15, 20, 22, 51, 61, 63, 69, 86–8, 94–5, 97
establishing a market presence abroad 84, 90, 93, 119; ways of 84–6
Euromobiliare 97
European Atomic Energy Community 27
European Coal and Steel Community 27
European Commission 30–1, 33, 36–9, 44, 52, 55–6, 58, 65–9, 71, 73–4, 82, 85, 92, 95, 99, 108–9; role and responsibilities 28–9
European Council 29; Hanover summit 40, 43; Madrid summit 113–14; Strasbourg summit 114
European council for payment systems 92
European Court of Justice 28, 68; role and responsibilities 30
European currency unit 5, 111–12; multicurrency system 114; single currency 110, 113
European Economic Community 27
European Free Trade Association 42
European investment bank 31
European monetary co-operation fund 111
European Monetary System 111, 115
European Parliament 28, 31–2, 39; role and responsibilities 29–30
European system of central banks 113–14
Exchange Rate Mechanism 112, 115
exchange rates 107, 112–13; fixed rates 110–11, 114

factoring 19, 61
Federal Reserve Board 66
finance houses 2
financial futures 3, 7, 9, 15, 17, 75
financial futures market 6, 75
Financial Services Act 3, 64, 68, 118, 120–1
First Banking Co-ordination Directive (1977) 46–8, 58, 69
first direct 97
First VAT directive (1969) 37
Foreign and Colonial 88
foreign exchange business 83, 90, 97
foreign exchange controls 3, 5–6, 9, 11, 13–15, 17–18, 20–1, 23, 50–4, 107–8, 117–18, 120
France 18, 21, 23–5, 28, 40, 42, 51, 53–4, 72, 79–80, 88–9, 94–7, 99, 108; banking system 8–9; bourse 9; francs 53
Frankfurt 4, 11–12, 120
freedom of establishment 46–9, 55, 58, 61, 65
freedom of provision of cross-border services 46–8, 50–1, 53, 55–6, 58–9, 65, 67, 74–5
free movement: of capital 27, 32, 39, 51, 53, 110; of goods 27, 32, 39, 51, 110, 116; of people 27,

29, 32, 51, 91, 110; of services 27, 32, 36, 39, 46, 51, 110, 116; prevention of 34–5
F von Lanschot Bankiers 94

G10 Committee 72
G30 Committee 4
General Agreement on Tariffs and Trade 42–3
Generale Bank 5, 88
Germany, West 14, 18, 21, 23–5, 28, 35, 50, 53, 60, 66, 72, 78, 83, 87–9, 94–6, 99–100, 108–9, 112; banking system 10–12; bundesbank 112; deutschmark 112
Greece 23, 28, 52, 54, 79, 95, 112; banking system 12–13
gross domestic product 24, 44–6, 103, 116

Hambros 96, 98
Hessiche Landesbank 89
Hill Samuel 96
home country 47, 59–60, 65, 70, 74, 83, 116; authorities 60, 64–5, 67, 71, 74; control 47, 55–6, 61, 63–4, 68, 75, 118, 120
host country 25, 59–60, 67, 74, 76, 116; authorities 56, 64–5; business conduct rules 64, 68, 75, 82; control 48–50, 63–4, 68, 72, 82, 117
Humberclyde Investment 88

Indonesia 87
inflation 33, 44, 110, 114–15
insurance 1, 7, 10–11, 13, 16, 19–20, 23–4, 37, 83, 87–9, 98–101, 103–4; companies 3, 5–8, 10–11, 14, 16, 19; life 3, 5, 8, 10, 14, 16, 19, 21, 98, 104; non-life 5, 8, 11, 16, 100
interest rates 13, 20–1, 64, 75, 80–1, 101, 107–9; adjustable 9; fixed 5, 9, 19, 54, 80; variable 5, 9, 16, 19, 54, 80–1
International Financial Services Centre 15
Ireland 23, 28, 52, 79, 108; banking system 13–15
Irish National Bank 13
Istitute Bancario San Paolo 96
Italy 14, 23, 28, 47, 49, 51, 53, 72, 83, 87, 94, 96–7, 99, 108, 112; banking system 15–17; lira 17, 112

Japan 28, 33, 42, 72, 77

Korea, South 33
Kredietbank 5

Landesbank Stuttgart 89
leasing 19, 22, 61, 88
letters of credit 83, 90
Lloyds Bank 1, 3, 92, 98
Lome Conventions 42
London 9, 66, 82, 108, 118, 120–1
London International Financial Futures Exchange 4, 12
London Traded Options Market 4
Luxembourg 24, 28–9, 53, 66, 81, 87, 99, 108–9; banking system 17–18; monetary association with Belgium 5, 53

Marché à Terme des Instruments Financiers 9
mergers and acquisitions/ takeovers 8, 10, 21, 63, 76, 83–6, 88–90, 93–8, 105–6, 118; cross-border M & A 85, 87–9, 96, 98, 119
Midland Bank 1, 3, 92, 97
minimum essential harmonization 36, 55–6, 61–3
money markets 3, 9, 20, 80–2, 101; discount money market 2; eurocurrency market 3, 5, 18; money market instruments 75
money transmission systems 91, 104
Morgan Grenfell 88, 96
mortgages 2–3, 5, 8, 11, 14, 19–21, 23, 80–3, 100; banks 10–11, 54; credit 5, 7, 9–10, 13, 16, 54, 61, 81, 100
mutual funds 10, 16, 18

mutual recognition of standards 36, 55–6, 60, 68
mutual societies 3

National Australia Bank 13
National Bank of Greece 12
national customs 54, 79, 90, 119
National Girobank 2
National Savings Bank 2, 59
national sovereignty 39, 109, 114–15
National Westminster Bank 1, 3, 13, 78, 83, 92, 94, 97–8
Nederlandse Credietbank 88
Netherlands 11, 23, 28, 35, 53, 66, 72, 78, 83, 88–9, 94, 96–7, 99, 108; banking system 18–19
New York 3, 9, 11
NMB Bank 89
non-EC countries 40, 42–3, 45, 53, 65–7, 71, 76–7, 113, 120 *see also* third countries

options 3, 15, 75
own funds 49, 58, 63, 69–70, 73; external elements 69–70; internal elements 69–70; Own Funds Directive 56, 68–70, 72

Paribas 87, 94
Paris 4, 6, 9, 80, 120
payment systems 90–2, 97
pensions 2, 7–8, 21, 98; pension funds 14, 18, 20, 23
Portugal 23, 28, 52, 79, 82–3, 87, 96, 112; banking system 19–21
Postal Savings Bank 19
Postbank 89
Post office 2
Post office giro institutions 58
Post office savings bank 13
price reductions: expected 101, 103–5; potential 101, 104–5
producer surplus, decline in 103
protectionism 33, 36, 40, 42, 66
Prudential Life company 98
prudential standards 50, 55, 63, 67–9, 72
public procurement 40, 44
Puget 97

Rabobank 18–19, 94
recommendation on deposit-guarantee schemes 56, 73–4
recommendation on monitoring and controlling large exposures 56, 73
reciprocity, reciprocal market access 40, 43, 65–7, 76, 88; effective market access 66–7; national treatment 66–7
regional policy 32, 110, 113
representative offices 25, 48, 83, 90, 95–6
retail banking, sector 2, 7–8, 10, 18, 20, 22–3, 47, 54, 78, 83–4, 87, 93–5, 97, 119–20
revaluation 111–12
risk 4, 15, 19, 69, 71, 73, 104; and return 107; contagion risk 63; credit risk 64, 71, 80; market risk 54, 64, 71–2; risk-hedging instruments 15, 75, 78; risk-weighted assets 8, 70–2
Rothschilds 96
Royal Bank of Scotland 1, 92, 95–6, 98

Scottish Equitable 98
Second Banking Co-ordination Directive (1989) 56, 58–68, 71, 75–6, 82, 120; criticisms of 67–8
securities 2, 6–7, 10, 12, 14, 18, 21, 52–3, 69, 75, 83, 100; securities trading 1, 4, 10, 50–1, 60–1, 64, 68, 75, 120
Selier 94
S G Warburg 96
Singapore 87
single administrative document 35
Single European Act (1987) 30, 32, 39–40, 113
Societé Générale 8, 88
solvency ratios 49–50, 58, 69, 71–2, 95; Solvency Ratio Directive 56, 64, 68, 70–2
Spain 28, 47, 50–3, 79, 82–3, 85, 87–9, 94–7, 99, 117; banking system 21–3

stock exchange 3–4, 7, 12, 15, 18, 20, 50–1, 68, 75–6; stock market 6, 22, 100, 118
subsidiaries 2, 8, 14, 25, 48, 60–1, 63, 65–6, 76, 85, 87–8, 95–7, 120
Sweden 42, 72
Switzerland 5, 43, 71–2, 87, 95, 109

Taiwan 33
takeover codes 85
tariffs 32, 42
tax, taxation 5, 7, 15, 19, 21, 32, 35, 37–9, 51, 109, 121; capital gains tax 15, 109; corporation tax 7, 15, 38; excise duties 37–8, 47; stamp duty 4; stock exchange turnover tax 12, 17; tax havens 17, 109; VAT 37–8, 47; withholding tax 6, 11–12, 17, 21, 38, 47, 107–9
third countries 35, 43, 65–7, 75, 118, 120 *see also* non-EC countries
Tokyo 3, 11
Toronto 6
Touche Remnant 88
trade position: external 33, 40–4; internal 33
treasury bills 9, 12–13, 20, 22
Treaty of Rome (1957) 27, 30, 32, 46, 50–1, 113
Trustees Savings Bank 2

Ulster Bank 13–14
United Kingdom 5, 8, 11, 14, 18, 21, 23–5, 28–9, 33, 35, 38, 40, 42, 49, 53–4, 59–60, 64, 66, 68, 72, 78–82, 85, 87–8, 92, 99–100, 103, 105, 108–9, 112, 114, 117–21; bank system 1–4; banks and 1992 strategies 93–8
United States of America 5, 14, 28, 33, 42, 66, 72, 77, 111
unit trusts 2, 52
universal banking, banks 6, 8, 10, 16–18, 23, 120–1

value added 24, 100–1, 104
Verenigde Spaarbank 89
voting system: qualified majority 29, 32, 39; simple majority 29; unanimity 29, 32–3, 39, 109

Westdeutsche Landesbank 11, 89
White Paper (1985) 33–9, 46–7, 52, 55
Wholesale banking, sector 2–3, 7, 10, 16, 22, 78, 82, 87, 93–4, 97, 119–20

Yorkshire Bank 88